The Language of Fiction

ONE WEEK

This accessible satellite text in the Routledge INTERTEXT series is unique in offering students hands-on practical experience of text analysis focused on fiction. Written in a clear, user-friendly style by an experienced teacher it combines practical activities with texts, followed by commentaries and suggestions for further activities. It can be used individually or in conjunction with the series core textbook, *Working with Texts: A core book for language analysis*.

Aimed at A-Level and beginning undergraduate students, *The Language of Fiction*:

- asks What is literature? How does it work? How do we read it?
- explores specific approaches to literary style and authorship
- deals with openings, point of view, speech, gender and pop fiction
- includes a wide range of literary extracts, from the classics of Hardy and Austen, to the contemporary works of Martin Amis, Angela Carter, Nick Hornby and Irvine Welsh
- has a comprehensive glossary of terms

Keith Sanger is a co-author of *Working with Texts: A core book for language analysis*. He is currently team leader for the NEAB English Language A Level and teaches English Literature, Language and Drama at New College, Pontefract.

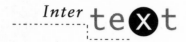

The Intertext series

◎ Why does the phrase 'spinning a yarn' refer both to using language and making cloth?

◎ What might a piece of literary writing have in common with an advert or a note from the milkman?

◎ What aspects of language are important to understand when analysing texts?

The Routledge INTERTEXT series will develop readers' understanding of how texts work. It does this by showing some of the designs and patterns in the language from which they are made, by placing texts within the contexts in which they occur, and by exploring relationships between them.

The series consists of a foundation text, *Working with Texts: A core book for language analysis*, which looks at language aspects essential for the analysis of texts, and a range of satellite texts. These apply aspects of language to a particular topic area in more detail. They complement the core text and can also be used alone, providing the user has the foundation skills furnished by the core text.

Benefits of using this series:

◎ **Unique** – written by a team of respected teachers and practitioners whose ideas and activities have also been trialled independently

◎ **Multi-disciplinary** – provides a foundation for the analysis of texts, supporting students who want to achieve a detailed focus on language

◎ **Accessible** – no previous knowledge of language analysis is assumed, just an interest in language use

◎ **Comprehensive** – wide coverage of different genres: literary texts, notes, memos, signs, advertisements, leaflets, speeches, conversation

◎ **Student-friendly** – contains suggestions for further reading; activities relating to texts studied; commentaries after activities; key terms highlighted and an index of terms

The series editors:

Ronald Carter is Professor of Modern English Language in the Department of English Studies at the University of Nottingham and is the editor of the Routledge INTERFACE series in Language and Literary Studies. He is also co-author of *The Routledge History of Literature in English*. From 1989 to 1992 he was seconded as National Director for the Language in the National Curriculum (LINC) project, directing a £21.4 million in-service teacher education programme.

Angela Goddard is Senior Lecturer in Language at the Centre for Human Communication, Manchester Metropolitan University, and was Chief Moderator for the project element of English Language A Level for the Northern Examination and Assessment Board (NEAB) from 1983 to 1995. Her publications include *The Language Awareness Project: Language and Gender*, vols I and II, 1988, and *Researching Language*, 1993 (Framework Press).

First series title:

Working with Texts: A core book for language analysis
Ronald Carter, Angela Goddard, Danuta Reah, Keith Sanger, Maggie Bowring

Satellite titles:

The Language of Sport
Adrian Beard

The Language of Newspapers
Danuta Reah

The Language of Advertising: Written texts
Angela Goddard

The Language of Humour
Alison Ross

The Language of Poetry
John McRae

The Language of Fiction
Keith Sanger

Related titles:

INTERFACE series:

A Linguistic History of English Poetry
Richard Bradford

Literary Studies in Action
Alan Durant and Nigel Fabb

Language, Literature and Critical Practice
David Birch

Dramatic Discourse
Vimala Herman

The Routledge History of Literature in English: Britain and Ireland
Ronald Carter and John McRae

English in Speech and Writing
Rebecca Hughes

The Language of Jokes
Delia Chiaro

Feminist Stylistics
Sara Mills

The Discourse of Advertising
Guy Cook

Language in Popular Fiction
Walter Nash

Inter te**x**t

The Language of Fiction

- Keith Sanger

LONDON AND NEW YORK

First published 1998
by Routledge
11 New Fetter Lane, London EC4P 4EE

Simultaneously published in the USA and
Canada
by Routledge
29 West 35th Street, New York, NY 10001

Typeset in Stone Sans/Stone Serif by
Solidus (Bristol) Limited

Printed and bound in Great Britain by
TJ International Ltd, Padstow, Cornwall

*British Library Cataloguing in Publication
Data*

A catalogue record for this book is
available from the British Library

*Library of Congress Cataloguing in Publication
Data*

Sanger, Keith, 1948–
    The language of fiction/Keith Sanger.
        p.   cm. –– (Intertext)
    Includes bibliographical references and
index.
    ISBN 0–415–14599–6 (pbk.)
    1. Fiction–Technique. I. Title. II. Series:
Intertext (London, England)
PN3355.S36   1988
808.3–dc21   97–20649
                                           CIP

ISBN 0–415–14599–6

For Kathryn and Ben

contents

acknowledgements

I'd like to thank Angie Goddard and Danuta Reah, especially for their comments during the drafting process; also Miranda Filbee, Jon Wells, Sara Sgarbi and Trinity College, Oxford.

The following texts and illustrations have been reprinted by courtesy of their copyright holders:

1   *The Magic Toyshop* by Angela Carter. Copyright © Angela Carter 1967. Reproduced by permission of the Estate of Angela Carter c/o Rogers, Coleridge & White Ltd, 20 Powis Mews, London W11 1JN

2   *Dirty Weekend* by Helen Zahavi. Reproduced by permission of Flamingo and David Grossman Literary Agency

3   *Money* and *London Fields* by Martin Amis. Reprinted by permission of the Peters Fraser and Dunlop Group Ltd

4   *On the Road* by Jack Kerouac, Penguin Books, 1972. Copyright © Jack Kerouac 1955, 1957. Reproduced by permission of Frederick Warne & Co. Also reproduced by permission of Sterling Lord Literistic, Inc. Copyright © 1957 by Jack Kerouac. Renewed 1986

5   *High Fidelity* by Nick Hornby. Reprinted by permission of Riverhead Books, a division of The Putman Berkley Group. Copyright © 1995 by Nick Hornby; also by permission of Victor Gollancz Ltd

6   *The Buddha of Suburbia* by Hanif Kureishi. Copyright © Hanif Kureishi 1990. Reproduced by permission of the author c/o Rogers, Coleridge & White Ltd, 20 Powis Mews, London W11 1JN, and the publishers Faber & Faber Ltd

7   *The Sound and the Fury* by William Faulkner. Reproduced by permission of Curtis Brown Group Ltd and Random House, Inc

8   *Paddy Clarke Ha Ha Ha* by Roddy Doyle. Reproduced by permission of Reed Books

9   *Down the Clinical Disco* by Fay Weldon. Reproduced by permission of Curtis Brown Group Ltd.

10 *Therapy* by David Lodge, reprinted by permission of Martin, Secker & Warburg and Curtis Brown Group Ltd

11 *Rites of Passage* by William Golding. Copyright © 1980 by William Golding. Reprinted by permission of Farrar, Straus & Giroux, Inc., and the publishers, Faber & Faber Ltd

12   *The Growing Pains of Adrian Mole* by Sue Townsend. Reproduced by permission of Curtis Brown Group Ltd, and Reed Books

13   *Lord of the Flies* by William Golding. Reprinted by permission of The Putman Publishing Group and Faber & Faber Ltd. Copyright © 1954 by William Golding; renewed © 1982 by William Golding

14   *A Small Good Thing* by Raymond Carver from *Short Cuts*, first published in Great Britain by Collins Harvill, 1993. Copyright © Tess Gallagher 1993. Reproduced by permission of The Harvill Press and International Creative Management, Inc.

15   *Brighton Rock* by Graham Greene. Reproduced by permission of David Higham Associates

16   *The Siege of Krishnapur* by J. G. Farrell. Reproduced by permission of Weidenfeld & Nicolson

17   *Lady Chatterley's Lover* by D. H. Lawrence. Used by permission of Laurence Pollinger Limited and the Estate of Frieda Laurence Ravagli

18   *The Secret Seven* by Enid Blyton. © 1949 Enid Blyton Ltd

19   *The Speckled Band* by Sir Arthur Conan Doyle. © 1996 Sheldon Reynolds. Reprinted by kind permission of Jonathan Clowes Ltd, London, on behalf of Sheldon Reynolds, administrator of the Conan Doyle copyright

20   *Heartbreaker* by Rosie Rushton. Taken from *Bliss* magazine, August 1996. Reproduced by kind permission of the author

21   *Generation X* by Douglas Coupland. Reproduced by permission of Little Brown

22   *The Wasp Factory* by Iain Banks. Reproduced by permission of Little Brown

23   Extract from *The New York Times*, 20 December 1922, p. 1, col. 3. Copyright © 1922 by The New York Times Co. Reprinted by permission

24   *Language Through Literature: An introduction* by Paul Simpson. © 1997 Paul Simpson. Reproduced by permission of Routledge

25   *Calvin and Hobbes* © Watterson. Distributed by Universal Press Syndicate. Reprinted with permission. All rights reserved

26   Extract from *In Our Time*, by Ernest Hemingway. Reprinted with permission of Scribner, a Division of Simon & Schuster. Copyright 1925 Charles Scribner's Sons. Copyright renewed 1953 by Ernest Hemingway.

The publishers have made every effort to contact copyright holders although this has not been possible in some cases. Outstanding permissions will be remedied in future editions. Please contact Moira Taylor at Routledge.

introduction

This book sets out to ask some questions of the language of fiction. It doesn't by any means either seek to give all the answers or cover the whole field of fiction writing. Certainly there already exist books which, in part, attempt to analyse in some depth some aspects of fiction.

What this book tries to do in one volume is to suggest some helpful ways into seeing how texts are constructed and how they might be read. It has tried to steer a line short of some excellent but arguably difficult academic books; it has tried to simplify and illustrate some of the 'big' areas in fiction. It has had very firmly in mind students of literature, language and communication and also their teachers who also may be looking for ways into the analysis of fictional texts.

This explains the structure of the units. Throughout there are suggestions for activities which either seek to raise questions or seek to provide practice in ideas already discussed in the unit. Commentaries normally follow these activities; these shouldn't be seen as model answers but as further exploration of the issues under question. At the end of each unit ideas for further investigation are given under extension work. Another idea behind the writing of this book was the aim of introducing a whole range of interesting texts. So the classics of Hardy and Austen rub shoulders with the writing of Coupland, Hornby and Welsh, *The New York Times* and the Frinton and Walton *Official Guide*.

The overall structure of the book has had in mind our first impressions of books when we come to read them. Hence the first unit is on openings; but it also starts to pose some questions about the attitude of the writer and the relationship established with the reader. Units 2 and 3 deal with the larger issues of internal and external point of view. Units 4 and 5 further explore writer choice in their depiction of character by focusing on representation of speech and then description. Unit 6 seeks to take a disciplined look at the romantic fiction of Mills and Boon and teenage magazines. Unit 7 closes the book with some final questions about literature and includes a very short story by Ernest Hemingway based on a news item as well as a comparison of a travel brochure with Anita Brookner's opening to *Hotel du Lac*.

It is suggested that students and teachers work through the first introductory unit which sets up a framework; this is then thoroughly explored in the next two units on point of view. After that, the units are more discrete so that if students and their teachers want some ways into the analysis of pop fiction, for example, then they can go straight to Unit 6.

Unit one

Openings

This book explores some of the ways prose fiction works, including how it presents its subject matter and how it relates to the reader. It seems a sensible, even obvious, place to begin by looking at some interesting openings. There are many reasons, of course, why we may start reading a book: it might have been recommended, it might be the book of the film we enjoyed, or it might be the book we've got to study, or even teach, as part of a course. But if we are casually browsing in a bookshop or library, advertising displays, jacket graphics and mind-watering blurbs might entice us to pick up a book and begin reading.

Openings are obviously important. They may do some or all of the following:

◎ seek to engage the reader
◎ give some indication of what kind of book this will be
◎ establish a relationship with the reader
◎ establish a voice
◎ establish a relationship with the subject matter.

Even the opening sentence might be revealing. Compare these opening sentences from two novels by the same author, Thomas Hardy:

> A Saturday afternoon in November was approaching the time of twilight, and the vast tract of unenclosed wild known as Egdon Heath embrowned itself moment by moment.
>
> *The Return of the Native*
>
> The schoolmaster was leaving the village, and everybody seemed sorry.
>
> *Jude the Obscure*

The opening sentence from *The Return of the Native* immediately establishes the importance of the 'vast tract of unenclosed wild known as Egdon Heath' which acts as a brooding presence in Hardy's novel, as important as any character. We are given the time, the season and a suggestion of atmosphere. Egdon Heath seems active - it 'embrowned itself' - and we might expect it to figure significantly throughout the book, as indeed it does.

The opening sentence from *Jude the Obscure*, on the other hand, refers to a character (yet without a name), an, as yet, indistinct character whose personality may, perhaps, be less important than his job of being a teacher. From this opening you might deduce that he will figure in the novel, but not as a major (or *the* major character).

In the opening to *Dombey and Son*, Charles Dickens introduces us to the two characters named in the title:

> Dombey sat in the corner of the darkened room in the great arm-chair by the bedside, and Son lay tucked up warm in a little basket bedstead, carefully disposed on a low settee immediately in front of the fire and close to it, as if his constitution were analogous to that of a muffin, and it was essential to toast him brown while he was very new.

Immediately we are presented with the two characters of the title, but not neutrally or without comment. Dickens uses the language of trade and business - 'Dombey ... and Son' - to suggest that the family relationship of father and son is rather businesslike. And Son (with a capital letter) is given a prominence both in context - father watching/guarding from the corner - and in sheer length of words, suggestive of the son's importance and his eventual inheriting of his father's fortune and business. Humour is also introduced in the analogy of or comparison between Son and a muffin being toasted.

We are made aware, then, of the writer's **attitude** and relationship to his created characters. By describing father and son as Dombey and Son they are made to seem less than flesh and blood, less credible perhaps and more like caricature, where one character trait is taken and exaggerated so that it becomes almost totally dominant. Dickens presents his characters, then, with a wry humour which continues in the next few sentences:

> Dombey was about eight-and-forty years of age. Son about eight-and-forty minutes. Dombey was rather bald, rather red ... Son was very bald, very red.

The contrasting of the two, like two sides of the same coin, is done by a balance using almost identical language and humour derived by suggesting a closeness between two very different time spans - years and minutes - and yet, despite this gap in age, they are both close in baldness and redness.

Activity

Read the opening sentence from each of these three novels. What impression do you get of the three characters introduced?

> 1 Emma Woodhouse, handsome, clever, and rich, with a comfortable home and happy disposition, seemed to unite some of the best blessings of existence; and had lived nearly twenty-one years in the world with very little to distress or vex her.
>
> 2 The summer she was fifteen, Melanie discovered she was made of flesh and blood.
>
> 3 This is the story of Bella, who woke up one morning and realised she'd had enough.

Commentary

In extract 1 (from *Emma* by Jane Austen) Emma wants for nothing: she's handsome (though now we would probably say attractive), clever and rich. Yet that word 'seemed' suggests doubt in the author's mind and warns us that, especially with little to vex her, perhaps she's not perfect. In fact Austen's heroine does make mistakes, meddles in other people's affairs, draws false conclusions and, in the process, hurts several innocent less well-disposed people. She, in fact, reflects Austen's comment that she wanted 'to take a heroine who no one will much like'. The presentation of Melanie in extract 2 (from Angela Carter's *The Magic Toyshop*) seems a much more tender and affectionate portrayal and, indeed, this attitude continues in the rest of the opening section of the novel. This line also suggests a coming of age, a rite of passage in the physical sense. A continuation of this opening, by the way, is given near the end of this unit.

Bella in extract 3 (from *Dirty Weekend* by Helen Zahavi), on the other hand, is a different proposition. Doesn't this sound like someone that you won't want to mess with? The short colloquial style of the sentence mirrors the decisive 'no messing' mind of the character. This opening, by the way, is interesting also because it draws attention to itself as a text: 'This is the story of . . .'.

Activity

Collect some opening sentences of your own. Do they reveal anything of the writer's attitude to his or her story or character(s)?

Voice

So far, then, in these few examples of opening sentences already given, we are seeing some kind of relationship or attitude that the author has towards their story and character(s). This attitude may be a sympathetic one, a detached one, an ironic one - whatever it is it will adopt a view, a stance, an opinion. This attitude is generally called **point of view** and, because it is such an important aspect of texts, it will be more fully discussed in the next two units. Another important, and useful, way of classifying the way texts are written is to try to describe the relationship writers have with their readers. Imagine, perhaps, the text being spoken. Can you hear what it sounds like? Can you describe it? In the sense that writers can be said to be speaking to their readers, then, this relationship can be called **voice**. Sometimes, of course, the voice of a writer can seem to be colourless or, perhaps better, toneless. The opening sentences of the two Hardy novels already quoted don't seem to have any particular timbre or quality. But the long, carefully constructed opening sentence from *Dombey and Son* suggests an intelligent, urbane voice and the wry humour in it suggests an intelligent wit too. On the other hand, the short direct address of *Dirty Weekend* suggests a voice that's saying 'right, here's a story; sit down and listen.' Don't worry if you wouldn't describe the voice here in quite these words; what is important is to start to be aware of its presence. Actually voice can be very difficult to describe but certainly, in *Dirty Weekend*, we are more conscious of the presence of the writer.

At this point it would be more illustrative to look at examples where an obvious voice is being adopted by the writer to tell the story. Sometimes the voice itself is more significant than the story and this is what engages the reader.

Activity

Look at these opening extracts from two very different novels. When you have read them, try to do two things: say what you think the writer's attitude is to the story and main character and try to describe the voice the writer is using.

Your father. You remember him in his faded blue pyjamas, giving you a ride on his back once, but it all seem so long ago. In school you call him 'Sir' like all the other children, and every Sunday you and Anthony take turns standing before him, watching him trim the nails on each hand you hold out, cutting clean and careful with sharp little scissors. At night you like watching him light the gas lamp, the blue flame from the methylated spirits gently burning, he pumping and pumping until the little net sac was full of light. And when he come back from his evening walks with his feet stretched out before him, you're always the first to loose out his lacings and take off his shoes. But he'd hardly ever touch you. Not like your mother tickling you till you had to beg her to stop, running her hands up and down your back and under your foot. Playing she was a spider.

Grace Nichols, *Whole of a Morning Sky*

As my cab pulled off FDR Drive, somewhere in the early Hundreds, a low-slung Tomahawk full of black guys came sharking out of lane and sloped in fast right across our bows. We banked, and hit a deep welt or grapple-ridge in the road: to the sound of a rifle-shot the cab roof ducked down and smacked me on the core of my head. I really didn't need that, I tell you, with my head and face and back and heart hurting a lot all the time anyway, and still drunk and crazed and ghosted from the plane.

'Oh man,' I said.

'Yeah,' said the cabbie from behind the shattered plastic of his screen. 'Fuckin A.'

My cabbie was fortyish, lean, balding. Such hair as remained scurried long and damp down his neck and shoulders. To the passenger, that's all city cabbies are - mad necks, mad rugs. This mad neck was explosively pocked and mottled, with a flicker of adolescent virulence in the crimson underhang of the ears. He lounged there in his corner, the long hands limp on the wheel.

'Only need about a hundred guys, a hundred guys like me,' he said, throwing his voice back, 'take out all the niggers and PRs in this fuckin town.'

I listened on my seat there. Owing to this fresh disease I have called tinnitus, my ears have started hearing things recently, things that aren't strictly auditory. Jet take-offs, breaking glass, ice scratched from the tray. It happens mostly in the morning but at other times too. It happened to me in the plane for instance, or at least I think it did.

'What?' I shouted. 'A hundred guys? That's not many guys.'

'We could do it. With the right gunge, we could do it.'

'Gunge?'

'Gunge, yeah. Fifty-sixes. Automatics.'

I sat back and rubbed my head. I'd spent *two hours* in Immigration, God damn it. I have this anti-talent for queues. You know the deal. Ho ho ho, I think, as I successfully shoulder and trample my way to the end of the shortest line. But the shortest line is the shortest line for an interesting reason. The people ahead of me are all Venusians, pterodactyls, men and women from an alternative timestream. They all have to be vivisected and bodybagged by the unsmiling 300-pounder in his lit glass box. 'Business or pleasure?' this guy eventually asked me. 'I hope business only,' I said, and meant it. With business I'm usually okay. It's pleasure that gets me into all this expensive trouble ... Then a half hour in customs, and another half before I firmed up this cab - yeah, and the usual maniac fizzing and crackling at its wheel. I've driven in New York. Five blocks, and you're reduced to tears of barbaric nausea. So what happens to these throwbacks they hire to do it all day for money? You try it.

I said, 'Why would you want to go and do a thing like that?'

'Uh?'

'Kill all the niggers and PRs?'

'They think, you know, you drive a yellow cab,' he said, and raised one limp splayed hand from the wheel, 'you must be some kind of a scumbag.'

I sighed and leaned forward. 'You know something?' I asked him. 'You really *are* a scumbag. I thought it was just a swearword until you came along. You're the first real one I've met.'

We pulled over. Rising in his seat he turned to me gradually. His face was much nastier, tastier, altogether more useful than I had banked on it being - barnacled and girlish with bright eyes and prissy lips, as if there were another face, the real face, beneath his mask of skin.

'Okay. Get out the car. I said out the fuckin car!'

'Yeah yeah,' I said, and shoved my suitcase along the seat.

'Twenty-two dollars,' he said. 'There, the *clock*.'

'I'm not giving you anything, scumbag.'

With no shift in the angle of his gaze he reached beneath the dashboard and tugged the special catch. All four door locks clunked shut with an oily chockful sound.

'Listen to me, you fat fuck,' he began. 'This is Ninety-Ninth and Second. The money. Give me the money.' He said he would drive me uptown twenty blocks and kick me out on the street, right there. He said that by the time the niggers were done, there'd be nothing left of me but a hank of hair and teeth.

I had some notes in my back pocket, from my last trip. I passed a twenty through the smeared screen. He sprang the locks and out I climbed. There was nothing more to say.

Martin Amis, *Money*

Commentary

The first extract recreates tender memories of the character's mother and father. It is unusual in two respects. First, it is addressed to the character — a young girl — and, secondly, the writing has some of the features of patwa — a creole spoken in Guyana. Both these aspects draw the writer closer to the central character and help to achieve a sympathetic portrayal of her.

So there is a constant reference to 'you' and 'your'; and verbs are used in the dialect form:

> it all seem so long ago
> he pumping and pumping
> when he come back

There is, too, an informality about the writing and sentence structure which suggests a personal and friendly voice:

> Your father
> Playing she was a spider

Short sentences mingle with longer ones and the language almost mimics a child's:

> clean and careful with sharp little scissors
> pumping and pumping until the little net sac was full of light

We are certainly meant to share in this gentle remembrance of childhood days.

Martin Amis's creation, John Self, is a real contrast. The language of the narrator is modern, 'now', very much at home in New York. Examples include 'FDR Drive', 'mad necks', 'mad rugs' meaning wild hair, 'firmed up', 'maniac fizzing'. Direct address to the reader is used, as in:

> I really didn't need that, I tell you
> I'd spent *two hours* in Immigration, God damn it ... You know the deal

Voice is perhaps more apparent when a character is speaking to the reader – and certainly when the character is opinionated as much as this one. Amis is here attempting to recreate the voice of a modern fast freak: the voice is confident, self-aware, cynical. His comments on others are acerbic: 'The people ahead of me are all Venusians, pterodactyls, men and women from an alternative timestream', and he boasts of his successful 'shoulder and trample' to the end of the shortest line. Yet we may approve of this anti-hero when he calls the cabbie a scumbag, in reaction to the racist comments about taking 'out all the niggers and PRs in this fuckin town'. PRs, by the way, is shorthand for Puerto Ricans.

Writers as writers

Before finishing this first unit you should also be aware of writers who draw attention to themselves, their writing or the actual craft of writing itself. Of course there's the classic 'Dear Reader …' address, but also a writer might choose to treat their characters as *real*, as if the writer's job is simply to record as faithfully as they can what actually *is*. Amis, in another novel, *London Fields*, writes of his main character:

I wish to Christ I could do Keith's voice. The *t*'s are viciously stressed. A brief guttural pop, like the first nanosecond of a cough or a hawk, accompanies the hard *k*. When he says *chaotic*, and he says it frequently, it sounds like a death rattle. 'Month' comes out as *mumf.* He sometimes says, 'Im feory …' when he speaks theoretically. 'There' sounds like *dare* or *lair*. You could often run away with the impression that Keith Talent is eighteen months old.

In *Dirty Weekend* and before getting into her stride in telling Bella's story, Zahavi draws attention to the craft of writing:

And now, the sketching in, the padding out, of what had gone before, of what it was that made her do the things she found she did.

(The juicy bits, the rank and lurid juicy bits, the bits that will make mothers warn their errant, toddler sons: Behave, or the Bella will get you - *those* bits come later.)

Activity

Finally, two more extracts. In the first, examine how Carter, in this fuller opening of *The Magic Toyshop*, establishes a girl's own sense of the wonder of growing up. And, in the second, from the opening of Mark Twain's *The Adventures of Huckleberry Finn*, look at how the writer establishes the voice of Huck Finn. The character of Finn even claims to be real and that the author didn't always tell the truth in his previous book. Note there is no commentary on this activity.

Extract 1

The summer she was fifteen, Melanie discovered she was made of flesh and blood. O, my America, my new found land. She embarked on a tranced voyage, exploring the whole of herself, clambering her own mountain ranges, penetrating the moist richness of her secret valleys, a physiological Cortez, da Gama or Mungo Park. For hours she stared at herself, naked, in the mirror of her wardrobe; she would follow with her finger the elegant structure of her rib-cage, where the heart fluttered under the flesh like a bird under a blanket, and she would draw down the long line from breast-bone to navel (which was a mysterious cavern or grotto), and she would rasp her palms against her bud-wing shoulder blades. And then she would writhe about, clasping herself, laughing, sometimes doing cartwheels and handstands out of sheer exhilaration at the supple surprise of herself now she was no longer a little girl.

Extract 2

You don't know about me, without you have read a book by the name of 'The Adventures of Tom Sawyer', but that ain't no matter. That book was made by Mr Mark Twain, and he told the truth, mainly. There was things which he stretched, but mainly he told the truth. That is nothing. I never seen anybody but lied, one time or another, without it was Aunt Polly, or the widow, or maybe Mary. Aunt Polly - Tom's Aunt Polly, she is - and Mary, and the Widow Douglas, is all told about in that book - which is mostly a true book; with some stretchers, as I said before.

Now the way that the book winds up, is this: Tom and me found the money that the robbers hid in the cave, and it made us rich. We got six thousand dollars apiece - all gold. It was an awful sight of money when it was piled up. Well, Judge Thatcher, he took it and put it out at interest, and it fetched us a dollar a day apiece, all the year round - more than a body could tell what to do with. The Widow Douglas, she took me for her son, and allowed she would sivilise me; but it was rough living in the house all the time, considering how dismal regular and decent the widow was in all her ways; and so when I couldn't stand it no longer, I lit out. I got into my old rags and my sugar-hogshead again, and was free and satisfied. But Tom Sawyer he hunted me up and said he was going to start a band of robbers, and I might join if I would go back to the widow and be respectable. So I went back.

The widow, she cried over me, and called me a poor lost lamb, and she called me a lot of other names, too, but she never meant no harm by it. She put me in them new clothes again, and I couldn't do nothing but sweat and sweat, and feel all cramped up. Well, then, the old thing commenced again. The widow rung a bell for supper and you had to come to time. When you got to the table you couldn't go right to eating, but you had to wait for the widow to tuck down her head and grumble a little over the victuals, though there warn't really anything the matter with them. That is, nothing only everything was cooked by itself. In a barrel of odds and ends it is different; things get mixed up, and the juice kind of swaps around, and the things go better.

Extension

1   Consolidate what you have learned in this unit by collecting some of your own openings. Then ask yourself three questions:

   ◎   Do you get a clear sense of character?
   ◎   Can you describe the author's attitude to the story or character(s)?
   ◎   Are you aware of a distinctive voice?

2   Write your own opening. Consider what you are trying to achieve. Do you succeed? (Give it to others to read.) You may also want to try this again after reading the next units on point of view.

Internal point of view

Two of the extracts used in the first unit - *Money* and *The Adventures of Huckleberry Finn* - are written in the *first person*; that is, the main character is telling the story from their point of view and of course using the 'I' form. This viewing of events largely through a character's eyes is called an *internal point of view*. We may not experience everything they do but events are mostly seen through their eyes, with an insight into their thoughts and feelings and often with comments on the situation. Extreme forms of this internal view would be the kind of writing which attempts to duplicate a running internal monologue of someone's loosely associated thoughts, also referred to as **stream of consciousness** writing. Some of Virginia Woolf's novels are composed in this style, as well as some of the writing in James Joyce's *Ulysses*. The absence of punctuation helps to intensify the sense of this being rather like someone's loosely associated thought, as in this made-up example:

> yes he said oh yes penalty penalty yes yes yes I can't look he said I can't oh Dicksy yes Dicksy you can do it oh god make him do it yes come on you irons oh yes Dicks please yes oh yes

Jack Kerouac's *On the Road,* charting his experiences travelling across America, is also worth noting. What makes this particularly interesting is that, although the writing is based on real events, the writing is charged with such strong personal reactions and feelings from the point of view of the narrator that, some would claim, it has many elements of the fictional about it. Kerouac called his form of writing spontaneous prose and his solution to stop his verbal flow from drying up when he needed to fit a new page was to tape together twelve-foot-long sheets of paper which he could feed into his typewriter in one single roll. In this way he finished his book in three weeks: a roll of paper typed as a single-spaced paragraph 120 feet long. Here are a few lines, just after he had set out from New York to make for San Francisco:

> In Newburgh it had stopped raining. I walked down to the river, and I had to ride back to New York in a bus with a delegation of school-teachers coming back from a weekend in the mountains - chatter-chatter blah-blah, and me swearing for all the time and the money I'd wasted, and telling myself, I wanted to go west and here I've been all day and into the night going up and down, north and south, like something that can't get started. And I swore I'd be in Chicago tomorrow, and made sure of that, taking a bus to Chicago, spending most of my money, and didn't give a damn, just as long as I'd be in Chicago tomorrow.

Incidentally, not everyone appreciates this form of writing. The American novelist Truman Capote, for instance, described Kerouac's work as 'Not writing, but typing'. Part of the problem, of course, is to do with the narrator trying to suggest the effect of fleeting and momentary observations while on the move; but another problem is to do with some people's views of where non-fiction ends and fiction begins.

Autobiographical fiction

This concern of what is real and what is created also affects texts which seem strongly autobiographical - **autobiographical fiction**. Openings along the lines of 'I'm going to tell you all about my life' have an assertiveness and self-awareness about them which mimics the style of the autobiography and suggests to the reader that the events to be recounted are true. Here is an opening, written in the style of J. D. Salinger's *The Catcher in the Rye*, which attempts to capture the definite voice of an angry and angst-ridden adolescent:

I suppose you want to know how it all happened, how it all started and all that 'when was the first time you felt the urge to hurt someone?' bullshit. Well I'm not gonna tell you. You'll just have to make that all up for yourself. And don't bother with all that 'parents are to blame' bullshit either. This is no Larkin 'they fuck you up your mum and dad'. My mum and dad were OK. Boring but OK. No it was all me. It was my idea that first killing. And I'm proud of it. So piss off with all that psychoanalytical stuff. Save it for the birds.

Note the colloquial and colourful language and the aggressive relationship the narrator adopts with the reader.

Activity

Here are two more autobiographically sounding extracts. First, from Nick Hornby's *High Fidelity*, where the narrator describes his first awareness and experience of girls; and, second, the opening of Jeanette Winterson's *Oranges Are Not The Only Fruit*. How do both these pieces give the impression that they are writing about childhood from the perspective of the adult looking back? How does the language and its ability, amongst other things, to evoke humour, convey the sense that this is adult writing, confident and self-assured?

15

Extract 1

We had no irony when it came to girls, though. There was just no time to develop it. One moment they weren't there, not in any form that interested us, anyway, and the next you couldn't miss them; they were everywhere, all over the place. One moment you wanted to clonk them on the head for being your sister, or someone else's sister, and the next you wanted to ... actually, we didn't know what we wanted next, but it was something, something. Almost overnight, all these sisters (there was no other kind of girl, not yet) had become interesting, *disturbing*, even.

I started going out with one of them ... no, that's not right, because I had absolutely no input into the decision-making process. And I can't say that she started going out with me, either: it's that phrase 'going out with' that's the problem, because it suggests some sort of parity and equality. What happened was that David Ashworth's sister Alison peeled off from the female pack that gathered every night by the bench and adopted me, tucked me under her arm and led me away from the swingboat.

... But ... on the fourth night of our relationship I turned up in the park and Alison was sitting on the bench with her arm around Kevin Bannister ...

And that was that. Where had I gone wrong? First night: park, fag, snog. Second night: ditto. Third night: ditto. Fourth night: chucked. OK, OK. Maybe I should have seen the signs. Maybe I was asking for it. Round about that second ditto I should have spotted that we were in a rut, that I had allowed things to fester to the extent that she was on the look-out for someone else. But she could have tried to tell me! She could at least have given me another couple of days to put things right!

Extract 2

Like most people I lived for a long time with my mother and father. My father liked to watch the wrestling, my mother liked to wrestle; it didn't matter what. She was in the white corner and that was that.
She hung out the largest sheets on the windiest days. She *wanted* the Mormons to knock on the door. At election time in a Labour mill town she put a picture of the Conservative candidate in the window.

She had never heard of mixed feelings. There were friends and there were enemies.

Enemies were: The Devil (in his many forms)
                 Next Door
                 Sex (in its many forms)
                 Slugs
Friends were: God
                 Our dog
                 Auntie Madge
                 The Novels of Charlotte Brontë
                 Slug pellets

and me, at first. I had been brought in to join her in a tag match against the Rest of the World. She had a mysterious attitude towards the begetting of children; it wasn't that she couldn't do it, more that she didn't want to do it. She was very bitter about the Virgin Mary getting there first. So she did the next best thing and arranged for a foundling. That was me.

I cannot recall a time when I did not know that I was special. We had no Wise Men because she didn't believe there were any wise men, but we had sheep. One of my earliest memories is me sitting on a sheep at Easter while she told me the story of the Sacrificial Lamb. We had it on Sundays with potato.

Commentary

Both extracts are able to look back at their childhood and summarize the situations and also comment on what was going on. Hornby in *High Fidelity*, for example, is able to view 'going out' with a girl as not really going out in the more adult understanding of the term. He didn't so much start going out with Alison – because that suggests he had some say in the matter – as that she adopted him when she 'peeled off from the female pack' and led him away. Within this adult perspective he evokes humour by using the language of young people in examples such as: 'One moment you wanted to clonk them on the head for being your sister, or someone else's sister' or when he describes the actual ritual of the dating process: 'First night: park, fag, snog. Second night: ditto. Third night: ditto. Fourth night: chucked'.

Similarly Winterson, in *Oranges Are Not The Only Fruit*, is able to look back at her upbringing and comment humorously on those times. First she parodies an obvious opening to an autobiography – 'Like most people I lived for a long time with my mother and father' – and then she proceeds to summarize her mother's character. She enjoys a good fight, 'She *wanted* the Mormons to knock on the door' and she even battled with the elements by hanging 'out the largest sheets on the windiest days'. With an adult perspective the mother's uncompromising stand on various points is neatly listed – under enemies and friends – and her fighting stance is highlighted with imagery from the world of wrestling – 'She was in the white corner' and 'I had been brought in to join her in a tag match against the Rest of the World'.

Activity

Now look at the opening of Hanif Kureishi's *The Buddha of Suburbia*, which is concerned with the narrator's sense of identity and growing up in the suburbs of London. How is it different to the two extracts above? Can you spot its more subtle hesitant approach?

> My name is Karim Amir, and I am an Englishman born and bred, almost. I am often considered to be a funny kind of Englishman, a new breed as it were, having emerged from two old histories. But I don't care – Englishman I am (though not proud of it), from the South London suburbs and going somewhere. Perhaps it is the odd mixture of continents and blood, of here and there, of belonging and not, that makes me restless and easily bored. Or perhaps it was being brought up in the suburbs that did it. Anyway, why search the inner room when it's enough to say that I was looking for trouble, any kind of movement, action and sexual interest I could find, because things were so gloomy, so slow and heavy, in our family, I don't know why. Quite frankly, it was all getting me down and I was ready for anything.

Commentary

There is an uncertainty, a kind of thinking on the page that is both different to the more strident opening of our angry adolescent above (p. 15) and different to the more confident and assured writing adopted by Hornby and Winterson. Kureishi here adopts a modest, self-effacing and disarmingly honest voice and the writing is hedged around with comments such as: 'Perhaps it is', 'Or perhaps it was' and 'I don't know why'.

A child's point of view

Sometimes, of course, writers choose to adopt the point of a view of a child and mimic the language of a child in the process. James Joyce's *A Portrait of the Artist as a Young Man* is interesting in that, as the novel progresses and the main character 'grows up', then so does the writing mature; the early passages try to recreate the language of a very young child and by the close we get a sense of an adult point of view. William Faulkner in his opening to *The Sound and the Fury* attempts to recreate the thoughts and perceptions of Benjy, a thirty-three-year-old man with the mind of a young child.

Activity

Read Faulkner's opening. How does the language suggest the idea of a simple mind?

Through the fence, between the curling flower spaces, I could see them hitting. They were coming toward where the flag was and I went along the fence. Luster was hunting in the grass by the flower tree. They took the flag out, and they were hitting. Then they put the flag back and they went to the table, and he hit and the other hit. Then they went on, and I went along the fence. Luster came away from the flower tree and we went along the fence and they stopped and we stopped and I looked through the fence while Luster was hunting in the grass.

Commentary

The extract, about a game of golf, is made up of a succession of short, simple sentences. It is a list of actions with frequent use of the conjunction 'and' and also repetition in syntax – 'Then they . . . Then they . . .', heavy reliance on pronouns and use of verbs without any sense of object, for example 'they were hitting ... and he hit and the other hit'. Add to this the simple use of terms, for example 'the flower tree', and we get something reminiscent of a young child's writing.

Activity

A naïve, childlike view can often be used for comic effect. In Roddy Doyle's *Paddy Clarke Ha Ha Ha*, Paddy, as a young boy, relates his childhood in Northern Ireland. Read this extract and note down how Doyle recreates a child's view. How does the humour work?

Father Moloney came into our class on the first Wednesday of every month. For a chat. We liked him. He was nice. He had a limp and a brother in a showband.

- In heaven, lads, he said, and waited. - In heaven you can live wherever and with whoever you like.

James O'Keefe was worried.

- Father, what if your mother doesn't want to live with you?

Father Moloney roared laughing but it wasn't funny, not really.

- Then you can go and live with her; it's quite simple.

- What if she doesn't want you to?

- She will want you to, said Father Moloney.

- She mightn't, said James O'Keefe. - If you're a messer.

- Ah there, you see, said Father Moloney. - There's your answer. There are no messers in heaven.

The weather was always nice in heaven and it was all grass, and it was always day and never night. But that was all I knew about it. My Granda Clarke was up there.

- Are you sure? I asked my ma.

- Yes, she said.

- Positive?

- Yes.

- Is he out of purgatory already?

- Yes. He didn't have to go there because he made a good confession.

- He was lucky, wasn't he?

- Yes.

I was glad.

My sister was up there as well, the one that died, Angela. She died before she came out of my ma but they'd had time to baptise her, she said, otherwise she'd have ended up in Limbo.

    - Are you sure the water hit her before she died? I asked my ma.

    - Yes.

    - Positive?

    - Yes.

I wondered how she managed, a not-even-an-hour-old baby, by herself.

    - Granda Clarke looks after her, said my ma.

    - Till you go up?

    - Yes.

Limbo was for babies that hadn't been baptised and pets. It was nice, like heaven, only God wasn't there. Jesus visited there sometimes, and Mary his mother as well. They had a caravan there. Cats and dogs and babies and guinea pigs and goldfish. Animals that weren't pets didn't go anywhere. They just rotted and mixed in with the soil and made it better. They didn't have souls. Pets did. There were no animals in heaven, only horses and zebras and small monkeys.

Commentary

Doyle recreates the impression of a child's point of view in various ways. First, the sentences are often short and simple, as in 'For a chat. We liked him. He was nice', or, if longer, heavily reliant on conjunctions, as in 'The weather was always nice in heaven and it was all grass, and it was always day and never night'. This list-like way of dealing with small chunks of thought at a time, not unlike Faulkner's writing, is reminiscent of children's writing; as is the use of zeugma, facts following each other apparently without connection, for example 'He had a limp and a brother in a showband'. Vocabulary is simple, as in the use of 'nice', and the constant questioning of his mother is typical, even using the same words – 'Are you sure? ... Positive?' There is a child-like sense of wanting to work it all out, to make sense of the adult world and asking, too, very awkward questions. Much of the humour is derived from the confident way Paddy tells us 'facts' about heaven, Limbo, and the fate of various animals. Perhaps the most amusing image is of Jesus and Mary visiting their caravan in Limbo. And why should 'horse and zebras and small monkeys' be so honoured? Humour also derives from the mixture of comment and dialogue, particularly in the exchange between Father Moloney and James O'Keefe. We get an image of a worried-looking James O'Keefe who has obviously been told by his mother that he's a 'messer', and the humour is reinforced both by the syntax – 'She mightn't, said James O'Keefe. – If you're a messer' – where we have to wait for his worried admission, and also by the glib response of Father Moloney.

For some practice in writing which recreates a child's point of view, continue the class discussion and Paddy's thoughts. Move on to a consideration of hell and imitate some of the features of writing that we have discussed here.

The X Generation

In *Generation X* Douglas Coupland attempts to create a voice of his generation, the 'twenty-somethings' culture, those born between 1961 and 1971. His characters take 'low-pay, low-prestige, low-benefit, no-future jobs in the service industry' – what he calls McJobs. His writing is full of the angst and jargon of the overeducated yet underemployed, and is interspersed with joky definitions in the margins. How does the language in the following extract from the book suggest this generation of 'twenty-somethings'?

Five days ago – the day after our picnic – Dag disappeared. Otherwise the week has been normal, with myself and Claire slogging away at our McJobs – me tending bar at Larry's and maintaining the bungalows (I get reduced rent in return for minor caretaking) and Claire peddling five-thousand-dollar purses to old bags.

Of course we wonder where Dag went, but we're not too worried. He's obviously just Dagged-out someplace, possibly crossing the border at Mexicali and off to write heroic couplets out among the saguaro, or maybe he's in LA, learning about CAD systems or making a black-and-white super-8 movie. Brief creative bursts that allow him to endure the tedium of real work.

And this is fine. But I wish he'd given some advance notice so I wouldn't have to knock myself out covering his tail for him, at work. He knows that Mr MacArthur, the bar's owner and our boss, lets him get away with murder. He'll make one quick joke, and his absence will be forgotten. Like the last time:

'Won't happen again, Mr M. By the way, how many lesbians does it take to put in a light bulb?'

Mr MacArthur winces. 'Dagmar, *shhh!* For God's sake, don't irritate the clientele!' On certain nights of the week Larry's can have its share of stool-throwing aficionados. Bar brawls, although colorful, only up Mr M's Allstate premiums. Not that I've ever seen a brawl at Larry's. Mr M is merely paranoid.

'Three - one to put in the light bulb and two to make a documentary about it.'

Forced laughter; I don't think he got it. 'Dagmar, you are very funny, but please don't upset the ladies.'

'But Mr MacArthur,' says Dag, repeating his personal tag line, 'I'm a lesbian myself. I just happen to be trapped in a man's body.'

This, of course, is an overload for Mr M, product of another era, a depression child and owner of a sizable collection of matchbook folders from Waikiki, Boca Raton and Gatwick Airport; Mr MacArthur who, with his wife, clips coupons, shops in bulk, and fails to understand the concept of moist microheated terry towels given before meals on airline flights. Dag once tried to explain 'the terry-towel concept' to Mr M: 'Another ploy dreamed up by the marketing department, you know - let the peons wipe the ink of thriller and romance novels from their fingers before digging into the grub. *Très* swank. Wows the yokels.' But Dag, for all of his efforts, might as well have been talking to a cat. Our parents' generation seems neither able nor interested in understanding how marketers exploit them. They take shopping at face value.

The monologue: 1

The mainstream and common format for internal first-person writing is of the kind where the writing is done as if addressed to a sympathetic reader. It will also tend to be written in the past tense and often written with reflection and perhaps with the end of the 'story' firmly in mind. Most of the extracts quoted in this unit, so far, are of this kind of mainstream writing. However, writers can adopt a form of writing which is much more like speech and written as if speaking to someone. This is the monologue (sometimes referred to as the dramatic monologue); it can be written in the present tense but it is rarely employed throughout a whole novel - though both Amis's *Money* (from Unit 1) and the

Salinger-inspired extract (from this unit) are written with some of the features associated with this form of writing.

Activity

Read this extract taken from a short story by Fay Weldon called *Down the Clinical Disco*. How does it suggest speech?

> You never know where you'll meet your own true love. I met mine down the clinical disco. That's him over there, the thin guy with the jeans, the navy jumper and the red woolly cap. He looks pretty much like anyone else, don't you think? That's hard work on his part, not to mention mine, but we got there in the end. Do you want a drink? Gin? Tonic? Fine. I'll just have an orange juice. I don't drink. Got to be careful. You never know who's watching. They're everywhere. Sorry, forget I said that. Even a joke can be paranoia.
>
> Let me tell you about the clinical disco while Eddie finishes his game of darts. He hates darts but darts are what men do in pubs, okay? The clinical disco is what they have once a month at Broadmoor. (Yes, that place. Broadmoor. The secure hospital for the criminally insane.) You didn't know they had women there? They do. One woman to every nine men. They often don't look all that like women when they go in, but they sure as hell look like them when (and if, if, if, if, if, if, if) they go out.

Commentary

Weldon positions the reader as if they were actually present with the author and *listening* to the monologue. So we get direct questions:

> He looks pretty much like anyone else, don't you think?
> Do you want a drink? Gin? Tonic?

There is a clear suggestion of the writer/speaker and reader/listener being in the same place from which to view the writer's 'true love' and there is also a suggestion of an interchange of dialogue between the writer/speaker and reader/listener: 'You didn't know they had women there? They do.' The use of the present tense also puts this extract firmly into the form of an actual on-going speech.

The monologue: 2

Of course not all monologue-type writing is as obviously directly addressed to the reader as this, or as obviously seeks to engage them as if in real conversation. Read this extract from David Lodge's *Therapy*. It still has the feel of a monologue about it though of course without the obvious positioning of the reader/listener as an actual presence sharing the same space as the writer/speaker and not being addressed directly or being asked questions. It is, though, framed in the present tense and does suggest speech in the way that details are filled in and added, in what is one long sentence. This is still, then, writing as if speaking to someone, and as if speaking to an imaginary, sympathetic ear.

I do as much of my banking as possible by a computerized phoneline system nowadays, and I send most of my letters by fax, or have Datapost call at the house if I have a script to mail, but occasionally I need some stamps and have to go and stand in one of those long Post Office queues with a lot of old biddies and single parents with snuffling infants in pushchairs waiting to collect their pensions and income support, and I can hardly restrain myself from shouting, 'Isn't it about time we had a counter for people who just want to buy stamps? Who want to *post* things? After all, this *is* a Post Office, isn't it?'

The journal

The journal or diary way of writing may be written in both the past and present tenses, though the past tense is more usual. It's writing as if being addressed to a sympathetic listener, though a better way to think of it might be to imagine it as more like silently talking to yourself. The writing is shaped by a self-editing process, a careful selection of what to record. Here are two examples which are quite different in their intentions. The first, from *Rites of Passage* by William Golding, is addressed to a named person and is very consciously aware of its form as a journal. The second, from *The Growing Pains of Adrian Mole* by Sue Townsend, is written with a delicious sense of fun, as the fifteen-year-old Mole tries to come to terms with his growing body, his parents and his love for Pandora. Entries are short and suggest the immediacy of quick jottings at the end of each day.

Extract 1

Honoured godfather,

 With those words I begin the journal I engaged myself to keep for you - no words could be more suitable!

 Very well then. The place: on board the ship at last. The year: you know it. The date? Surely what matters is that it is the first day of my passage to the other side of the world; in token whereof I have this moment inscribed the number 'one' at the top of this page. For what I am about to write must be a record of our *first day*. The month or day of the week can signify little since in our long passage from the south of Old England to the Antipodes we shall pass through the geometry of all four seasons!

Extract 2

Sunday May 9th: I have just realised that I have never seen a dead body or a real female nipple. This is what comes of living in a cul-de-sac.

 Monday May 10th: I asked Pandora to show me one of her nipples but she refused. I tried to explain that it was in the interests of widening my life experience, but she buttoned her cardigan up to the neck and went home.

 Wednesday May 12th: I received the following letter from Pandora this morning:

 Adrian,

 I am writing to terminate our relationship. Our love was once a spiritual thing. We were united in our appreciation of art and literature, but Adrian you have changed. You have become morbidly fixated with my body. Your request to look at my left nipple last night finally convinced me that we must part.

 Thursday May 13th: Yesterday before I opened *that* letter I was a normal type of intellectual teenager. Today I know what it is to suffer ... I love her! Oh God! Pandora! ...

> *Friday May 14th:* Why oh why did I ask Pandora to show me *her* nipple? Anybody's nipple would have done. Nigel says that Sharon Botts will show *everything* for 50p and a pound of grapes.
>
> *Saturday May 22nd:* My father has just asked me if I would like a sister or a brother. I said neither. Why do they keep drivelling on about kids? I hope they aren't thinking of adopting one. They are terrible parents. Look at me. I'm a complete neurotic ...
>
> *Thursday July 1st:* Nigel has arranged for me to have a blind date with Sharon Botts. I am meeting her at the roller skating rink on Saturday. I am dead nervous. I don't know how to roller-skate, let alone make love.

Finally

We would expect the first-person narrative to encourage a sympathetic link between reader and narrator and, indeed, this is normally so. However, there are some interesting examples where, because of the behaviour, attitude or language of the narrator, this is not the case. We might cite the speaker John Self in Amis's *Money* as someone of whom we don't thoroughly approve - a kind of anti-hero. The same might be said of Iain Banks's narrator in *The Wasp Factory,* who tells us:

> Two years after I killed Blyth I murdered my young brother Paul, for quite different and more fundamental reasons than I'd disposed of Blyth, and then a year after that I did for my young cousin Esmerelda, more or less on a whim. That's my score to date. Three. I haven't killed anybody for years, and don't intend to ever again. It was just a stage I was going through.

If you have the time, then David Lodge's *Therapy* is worth a closer look. In this book Lodge adopts the role of different characters who, naturally, don't only use different voices but also different forms of writing. Much of the book is narrated by the main character Laurence 'Tubby' Passmore (who, as it turns out, conveniently happens to be a TV scriptwriter) and concerns, amongst other things, the break-up of his marriage and his subsequent quest for fulfilment. At intervals different characters in his life give accounts of events, but then the narrator Passmore 'comes clean' and announces that he wrote their narratives too; of course the narrator is able to do this because he adopts different voices. Here is a flavour. In this extract we get an account by Amy, a long-term friend of Laurence, who agrees, for the first time, to go away with him for a short break to Tenerife. She is talking to her analyst.

It's extraordinary how as soon as you have to share space with somebody, you begin to see them in a completely different light … Well, the bathroom was windowless, as they usually are in modern hotels, and the extractor fan didn't seem to be working, at least it wasn't making any kind of noise, so I made sure I used the bathroom first after breakfast. It won't surprise you in the light of our previous discussions about toilet training that, how shall I put this, that when I manage to do number twos the stools are rather small, hard, dense little things. Are you sure you want me to go on? Well, the fact is that the Tenerife toilet simply couldn't cope with them. When I pulled the chain they danced about merrily in the water like little brown rubber balls, and refused to disappear. I kept pulling the chain and they kept bobbing back to the surface. Talk about return of the repressed. I got quite frantic. I just couldn't leave the bathroom until I got rid of them. I mean, it's not very pleasant to find someone else's turds floating in the toilet just as you're going to use it, and it certainly puts a damper on romance, wouldn't you say? I couldn't bring myself to apologize or explain to Laurence, or make a joke of it. You have to be married to somebody for at least five years to do that. What I really needed was a good bucket of water to slosh into the toilet bowl, but the only container in the bathroom was a waste-paper bin made of plastic latticework. Eventually I got rid of my little pellets by pushing them round the U-bend one by one with the toilet brush, but it's not an experience I would care to repeat.

Later in the book the overall narrator, Laurence Passmore, who is keeping a journal of events, admits that he also wrote Amy's account. He writes:

The bit about her sewage-disposal problems in the Playa de las Americas hotel was an extrapolation from listening to her endlessly cranking the handle of the toilet when she was in the bathroom.

Extension

1   Collect other interesting examples of autobiographical fiction, monologues and journal/diary writing. Salinger's *The Catcher in the Rye* is certainly worth reading.
2   Consider doing some of your own writing from the point of view of an adult looking back confidently, and knowingly, on earlier times.
3   Consider writing about the same events from different points of view, and perhaps using different forms, for example, journal form, telephone format etc.
4   Find other examples where we may be less than sympathetic to the narrator. Anthony Burgess's *A Clockwork Orange* is worth looking at. Also consider constructing your own unlikeable narrator.

External point of view

What could be considered the opposite of first-person internal point of view writing is writing in the third person, that is using the 'he/she/they' form; this kind of writing would seem to be naturally associated with an *external point of view*. An external point of view, in its extreme form, would be one where events are viewed dispassionately and without any insight into a character's feelings. A news report would be just such an example – 'The accused were seen leaving the site of the theft at 8.10 pm ...'. To take an example from prose fiction, William Golding, in his opening to *Lord of the Flies* adopts this external point of view:

> The boy with fair hair lowered himself down the last few feet of rock and began to pick his way towards the lagoon. Though he had taken off his school sweater and trailed it now from one hand, his grey shirt stuck to him and his hair was plastered to his forehead.

Here the boy's physical state and actions are viewed and described objectively and there is no insight into his feelings or thoughts. As might be expected, this form of writing is difficult to sustain throughout a whole novel (Golding does, in fact, vary his point of view in *Lord of the Flies*) so that where we find most examples is, perhaps not surprisingly, in the short story. Ernest Hemingway is often quoted as one of the finest or purest exponents of the external point of view and, if you want to look now at one of his short stories that does just this, then turn to Unit 7. The (very) short story given there is closely based on a news item from the *New York Times* and, as such, might be expected to be primarily concerned with fact.

Even so, the external point of view is rarely employed exclusively even in writers prone to using it. This extract from Raymond Carver, best-known as a skilful exponent of the short story genre, is perhaps typical of its use:

Saturday afternoon she drove to the bakery in the shopping center. After looking through a loose-leaf binder with photographs of cakes taped onto the pages, she ordered chocolate, the child's favorite. The cake she chose was decorated with a space ship and launching pad under a sprinkling of white stars, and a planet made of red frosting at the other end. His name, SCOTTY, would be in green letters beneath the planet. The baker, who was an older man with a thick neck, listened without saying anything when she told him the child would be eight years old next Monday. The baker wore a white apron that looked like a smock. Straps cut under his arms, went around in back and then to the front again, where they were secured under his heavy waist. He wiped his hands on his apron as he listened to her. He kept his eyes down on the photographs and let her talk. He let her take her time. He'd just come to work and he'd be there all night, baking, and he was in no real hurry.

Raymond Carver, *A Small Good Thing*

Much of this is written from the point of view of the detached observer. There is an account of actions: driving to the bakery, looking through a loose-leaf binder of cakes, the baker listening without saying anything, wiping his hands on his apron, etc.; there is also description: for example of the cake and the baker's apron. Writing, however, totally from this point of view would be difficult to sustain; certainly it would be difficult to engage the reader. There are, then, in this extract, some things the detached observer could not report; can you spot them? One is the fact that chocolate is the child's favourite; another is that the baker was in no real hurry. These facts could only be known with extra information that surveillance camera observation could not provide. To know, for example, that the baker was in no hurry, the writer has to have access to the baker's thoughts and feelings. You might well have picked out other facts too: for example, knowing that the baker was an older man, perhaps, or knowing that he would be there all night baking.

Activity

Now try your hand at writing like a detached observer, just reporting the facts and making no comment. An area where reporting of this nature, without speculation, is desirable, is in the court room. Imagine you are in the police force; present a report of the incident from the opening of *Money*, given in Unit 1, that involves the cab, the driver and his fare. If it helps, imagine you are a fly-on-the-wall or hidden camera in the cab.

Note there is no commentary on this activity.

An unframed window

So, to sum up so far: the external point of view is like an unframed window on events which are reported dispassionately, objectively and without comment. In its purest or extreme form there is:

◎ no insight into a character's feelings
◎ no authorial comment
◎ no awareness of the author.

Here are two more examples from Graham Greene's *Brighton Rock*, which revolves around the criminal underworld of the 1930s in this south-coast resort. When we first meet Pinkie, the seventeen-year-old leader of a small gang, he is introduced with a detached external point of view which is entirely appropriate to his character. He is cold and emotionless; Greene describes him thus: 'his grey eyes had an effect of heartlessness like an old man's in which human feeling has died'. Anyway, Hale has just arrived in Brighton – the book opens with the dramatic lines: 'Hale knew, before he had been in Brighton three hours, that they meant to murder him' – and he is drinking in a pub.

> The gin slopped out of Hale's glass onto the bar. A boy of about seventeen watched him from the door - a shabby smart suit, the cloth too thin for much wear, a face of starved intensity, a kind of hideous and unnatural pride.

Some of this reads like an account in a court room - factual and without comment - but note the additional description of the face and the mention of a 'hideous and unnatural pride'. This is information extra to what an external point of view would give; if this was reported in court a barrister might well object that this is not fact but speculation or opinion.

Activity

Just to make sure you've got the idea, have a look at another extract from *Brighton Rock*. Note the external point of view at work; but can you spot what might be construed as speculation or comment by the author?

> In front of the chairs the men strolled in twos and threes, wearing their summer suits for the first time, knife-edged silver-grey trousers and elegant shirts; they didn't look as if they cared a damn whether they got a girl or not, and among them Hale went in his seedy suit and his string tie and his striped shirt and his inkstains, ten years older, and desperate for a girl. He offered them cigarettes and they stared at him like duchesses with large cold eyes and said, 'I don't smoke, thank you,' and twenty yards behind him he knew, without turning his head, that Cubitt strolled.

Commentary

Much of this writing is external point of view: the men strolling in twos and threes, the description of the clothes of the men, Hale's clothes, his offering of cigarettes and the replies of the girls. However, comment or speculation is offered in:

they didn't look as if they cared a damn whether they got a girl or
not
they stared at him like duchesses with large cold eyes.

We are also given an insight into Hale's mind:

[He was] desperate for a girl
and twenty yards behind him he knew, without turning his head,
that Cubitt strolled.

You might have suggested that describing the shirts as 'elegant' is
comment; it probably is. This illustrates the fact that even in what
appears to be detached external point of view writing there are often
extra bits of information, which at first we may not be conscious of,
which add comment and reveal something of a character's feelings.

Free direct thought

Most third-person writing is a mixture of different views and some
writers can exploit their various positions in subtle yet complex ways.
Some positions which writers adopt include:

◎   being closely linked to one character
◎   being omniscient (all-seeing)
◎   offering comments on the art of writing
◎   offering comments on life in general.

Writing in the third person gives the author the freedom to do all of these
things but being able to always spot what's going on is actually a lot
trickier than we might suppose. With first-person writing, for example,
we can assume that the point of view is internalized, but some third-
person point of view writing - not a whole text but perhaps the odd
word, line or sentence - can be just as internalized as the first person form.
Free direct thought is such an accepted way of writing that we don't
notice it; in fact it's only when it's absent - as in some of the work of
Ernest Hemingway and Raymond Carver - in the extreme external point
of view that we perhaps become aware of its style.
    Some of Jane Austen's writing is perhaps the finest example of
internalized third-person writing; finest in the sense that the
internalized parts melt seamlessly into the more detached third-person
narration. As a way in, however, let us start with a text which is more

35

accessible (and which we have already used): Helen Zahavi's *Dirty Weekend*. Zahavi's heroine, Bella, wakes up one morning and decides she's had enough of being stepped on, spied upon and abused by men, and over the weekend of the title she takes revenge. For this she needs a gun. At the opening of Chapter Nine Bella has just failed to buy a gun from a gun shop - she has no licence for one - and is walking away from the shop in anger. Imagine you have written the first paragraph, then consider your options for the second. Here's the first paragraph:

> She stood outside the shop with light flakes of snow falling on her bare head. Deflated. The momentum suddenly halted. The adrenalin gradually leaking away. She began walking down the road, going nowhere.

Now consider these four options for starting the second paragraph:

1   She carried on walking down the road.
2   She looked angry.
3   She was angry.
4   She thought, damn them.

We're concerned not with what sounds better or which option Zahavi herself might have chosen, but in presenting these different options showing how, as we move from option 1 to option 4, the writing moves from an external point of view to more internalized points of view. The options could be labelled like this:

1   She carried on walking down the road - *external*
2   She looked angry - *external but with speculation and comment*
3   She was angry - *internal*
4   She thought, damn them - *internal with actual inner voice/thoughts*

The kind of writing that option 3 is an example of - access to a character's feelings - is part and parcel of most third-person writing and, when there is one main character, this access is often *only* to their feelings. What, perhaps, is more difficult to be aware of is the quality and depth of access that option 4 suggests, that is the actual quoting of a person's thoughts. If we decide to choose option 4 for the start of paragraph two – 'She thought, damn them' – but don't want to bother with the words 'She thought' – because it's clumsy or obvious that we've got Bella's thoughts – then we could just write:

Damn them.

and this way of presenting a character's thoughts is called *free direct thought*. It's free direct thought which can often mark out the more subtle types of third-person writing and is a deeper level of access to a character's internal point of view. Zahavi, in fact, does choose to write her second paragraph as if we could hear Bella's thoughts. Here, then, are her first two paragraphs:

> She stood outside the shop with light flakes of snow falling on her bare head. Deflated. The momentum suddenly halted. The adrenalin gradually leaking away. She began walking down the road, going nowhere.
>
> Damn them. Damn them all. Damn all the legislators with their well-protected privacy. Damn them to hell and back, and damn their lousy gun-licences.

So we get Bella's direct thoughts; we are very much inside her head, hearing what she is thinking. This internalised way of writing is both dramatic and an efficient way of revealing the heroine's feelings.

Now for Jane Austen. As might be expected, where there is one central character we might expect more internal point of view, and *Emma* is no exception. Although the language is more difficult Austen is doing essentially what Zahavi does.

First an extract where we are clearly made aware of the heroine's feelings. Emma is returning home alone with Mr Elton after a dinner at which he has had rather too much to drink. Emma has been encouraging Mr Elton to look on her adopted friend Harriet Smith as a prospective wife. She has failed to see, however, that it is she whom Mr Elton wants. On first reading we, seeing some of the events through Emma's eyes, are also unaware of his real intentions. On a second reading, however, some of the ambiguous incidents start to make more sense. 'Making violent love' by the way means '*expressing* his love' here.

> To restrain him as much as might be, by her own manners, she was immediately preparing to speak with exquisite calmness and gravity of the weather and the night; but scarcely had she begun, scarcely had they passed the sweep-gate and joined the other carriage, than she found her subject cut up – her hand seized – her attention demanded, and Mr Elton actually making violent love to her.

We are aware of Emma's state of mind – she was 'preparing to speak with exquisite calmness' – and we get her view of Mr Elton's advances – 'making violent love to her'. Presumably, his view of events would be quite different. Writing in the third person but from Mr Elton's point of view we might get something like:

> At last he had her to himself. Emma began to talk about the weather but, on impulse, he took her exquisite hand and told her of his love.

A way of seeing how internalized Austen's original extract is would be to see how easy it would be to turn this writing into first-person monologue. If we replace all the third-person pronouns which relate to Emma with the first person, the passage would then read:

> To restrain him as much as might be, by *my* own manners, *I* was immediately preparing to speak with exquisite calmness and gravity of the weather and the night; but scarcely had *I* begun, scarcely had *we* passed the sweep-gate and joined the other carriage, than *I* found *my* subject cut up – *my* hand seized – *my* attention demanded, and Mr Elton actually making violent love to *me*.

So, although the original extract is written in the third person it actually represents the character's own point of view and mimics her own language. Just by changing the appropriate pronouns from third to first person this piece could then quite easily read like a monologue or journal. This kind of writing, then, is very internalized.

Look at another extract a little later in the book as Emma reflects on Mr Elton's behaviour:

> But - that he should talk of encouragement, should consider her as aware of his views, accepting his attentions, meaning (in short) to marry him! - should suppose himself her equal in connection or mind! - It was most provoking.

If, again, we replace the third-person pronouns which relate to Emma with the first person we would get:

> But - that he should talk of encouragement, should consider *me* as aware of his views, accepting his attentions, meaning (in short) to marry him! - should suppose himself *my* equal in connection or mind! - It was most provoking.

This new version could almost be Emma actually talking; the exclamation marks intensify her outrage; it now reads like a dramatic monologue. Austen, then, is writing in the form that the character might use if writing a first-person monologue.

Some critical books that you may come across may try to differentiate between indirect speech and indirect thought. This fine tuning between the two terms is really a very fine line. What's important is to try to be aware of this technique that some writers employ of cutting closer to a character's feelings by actually giving their thoughts; in doing so the writer switches from an apparently external view to a very intimate recording of the character's actual thoughts. Sometimes this is even rendered as a kind of internal monologue - hence the term of indirect speech that is sometimes used. This is a really a matter of voice: are we hearing the character's thoughts or a kind of spoken monologue? Just try to be aware of the subtle switch into a character's mind and thoughts or potential speech.

Omniscient author

Writers may choose to stay with their character, observing them from within and without, describing only the incidents in which they participate and revealing nothing of incidents where they are not present; *Emma* is just such a novel. Other writers may choose to act the **omniscient author**, able to look at all events involving different characters; Dickens does this, entering the heads of many characters and commenting on them too.

Writers also can and do vary their point of view and voice within the same novel, chapter or, sometimes quite subtly, within the same sentence.

Activity

Look at this edited version of the opening chapter of Zahavi's *Dirty Weekend*. There are examples here, amongst other things, of (1) the author directly addressing the reader, (2) giving insights into Bella's feelings, and (3) also offering views on life in general (the philosophical voice). The relevant lines are italicised. Can you match the lines to these different positions of the author?

This is the story of Bella, who woke up one morning and realised she'd had enough.

She's no-one special. *You must have seen them. You've probably passed them. You've certainly stepped on them.*

She could have done the decent thing. She could have done what decent people do. She could have filled her gently rounded belly with barbiturates, or flung herself, with gay abandon, from the top of a tower block. They would have thought it sad, but not unseemly. Alas, poor Bella, they would have said, as they shovelled what remained of her into the waiting earth.

But pain and Bella made poor companions. She ran from pain, and thought it wouldn't find her. There might have been another reason why she couldn't do the deed. Another reason why she carried on, regardless. Perhaps it was the thought of having been, and gone, and left no mark. The thought that if she finished it, she would have had no story. The thought that no-one even knew her name. For though she barely was alive, she wanted them to know her name. She wanted them, if nothing else, at least to know her name.

Some people are good at life, and some are bad. Bella was bad. No-one had taught her how to do it, so she stumbled along in the dark. *All she wanted was to be left alone*, which didn't seem a lot to ask. And nothing would have changed, no-one would have known her name, but for the man who watched her. He saw her in her basement, and had to have a go. He didn't have the sense to let her be.

He thought she was an empty vessel that he alone could fill. He thought he'd take her by the hair and pull her through the street. He thought he'd clamp a hand across her mouth, and bend her into what he wanted. His trouble was he thought too much. A little mind with big ideas.

For Bella couldn't bend.

As he found out, as she found out, Bella could only break.

Commentary

Zahavi ranges widely in this opening chapter. The lines 'You must have seen them. You've probably passed them. You've certainly stepped on them' are directly addressed to the reader. The paragraph beginning 'But pain and Bella made poor companions' and the line 'All she wanted was to be left alone' give an insight into Bella's feelings, while the line 'Some people are good at life, and some are bad' is the author adopting a philosophical comment about life in general.

Zahavi, however, also adopts other positions here. The voice of the story-teller, or writer consciously present as writer, is apparent at three points:

This is the story of Bella
And nothing would have changed
As he found out, as she found out, Bella could only break.

We also get insights into the man's mind in the paragraph beginning 'He thought she was an empty vessel that he alone could fill.' Finally Zahavi pretends to voice the opinion of other people, which is a sort of unsympathetic, 'public' voice in the lines beginning 'She could have done the decent thing'.

This opening is unusual in its range of points of view, but a close reading is valuable in showing how easily and smoothly different stances can be adopted.

Activity

Read this next extract, from. J. G. Farrell's *The Siege of Krishnapur* which deals, amongst other things, with the British in India during the nineteenth century and the keeping of a stiff upper lip in a small fort under Indian siege. This particular extract concerns two men – Harry and Fleury (also known as 'Dobbin') – acting as heroes in saving a young lady, Lucy, who has been attacked by a swarm of cockchafers (flying insects). There are three different points of view at work. It opens with authorial description and comment, then moves to view events from the point of view of Harry and Fleury and then, finally, ends with a view of events from the new entrants to the scene. Try to locate the changes.

Poor Lucy! Her nerves had already been in a bad enough state. She leapt to her feet with a cry which was instantly stifled by a mouthful of insects. She beat at her face, her bosom, her stomach, her hips, with hands which looked as if they were dripping with damson jam. Her hair was crawling with insects; they clung to her eyebrows and eyelashes, were sucked into her nostrils and swarmed into the crevices and cornices of her ears, into all the narrow loops and whorls, they poured in a dark river down the back of her dress between her shoulderblades and down the front between her breasts. No wonder the poor girl found herself tearing away her clothes with frenzied fingers as she felt them pullulating beneath her chemise; this was no time to worry about modesty. Her muslin dress, her petticoats, chemise and underlinen were all discarded in a trice and there she stood, stark naked but as black and glistening as an African slave-girl. How those flying bugs loved Lucy's white skin!

Any moment now she would faint. But they could hardly dash forward and seize her with their bare hands. Or could they? Would it be considered permissible in the circumstances? But while they hesitated and debated, Lucy's strength ebbed away and she fell in a swoon, putting to death a hundred thousand insects beneath her lovely body. There was nothing for it but for the two young men themselves to go to Lucy's aid so, clearing their minds of any impure notions, they darted forward and seized her humming body, one by the shoulders, the other by the knees. Then they carried her to a part of the banqueting hall where the flying bugs were no longer ankle deep. But now they were faced with another predicament, how to remove the insects from her body?

It was Fleury who, remembering how he had made a visor for his smoking cap, found the solution by whipping his Bible out of his shirt and tearing the boards off. He gave one of these sacred boards to Harry and took the other one himself. Then, using the boards as if they were giant razor blades, he and Harry began to shave the black foam of insects off Lucy's skin. It did not take them very long to get the hang of it, scraping carefully with the blade at an angle of forty-five degrees and pausing from time to time in order to wipe it clean. When they had done her back, they turned her over and set to work on her front.

Her body, both young men were interested to discover, was remarkably like the statues of young women they had seen ... like, for instance, the Collector's plaster cast of *Andromeda Exposed to the Monster*, though, of course, without any chains. Indeed, Fleury felt quite like a sculptor as he worked away and he thought that it must feel something like this to carve an object of beauty out of the primeval rock. He became quite carried away as with dexterous strokes he carved a particularly exquisite right breast and set to work on the delicate fluting of the ribs. The only significant difference between Lucy and a statue was that Lucy had pubic hair; this caused them a bit of a surprise at first. It was not something that had ever occurred to them as possible, likely, or even, desirable.

'D'you think this is *supposed* to be here?' asked Harry, who had spent a moment or two scraping at it ineffectually with his board. Because the hair, too, was black it was hard to be sure that it was not simply matted and dried insects.

'That's odd,' said Fleury, peering at it with interest; he had never seen anything like it on a statue. 'Better leave it, anyway, for the time being. We can always come back to it later when we've done the rest.'

But at that moment there was a noise behind them and both young men turned at once. There stood Louise, Miriam, and the Padre, gazing at them with horror.

'Harry!'

'Dobbin!'

The Padre was unable to find any word at all; his eyes had come to rest on the golden letters 'Holy Bible' on the back of Fleury's razor blade.

'You couldn't have come at a better time,' said Fleury cheerfully. 'Harry and I were just wondering how we were going to get her clothes on again.'

Commentary

The first paragraph is largely authorial description and comment. The intensity of the attack by the cockchafers is largely told from an external point of view – 'Her hair was crawling with insects ... they poured in a dark river down the back of her dress' – and so on. There is, though, some indication of how she is feeling – 'she felt them pullulating beneath her chemise' – but overall we witness the incident as observers. Farrell adds comment such as 'Poor Lucy!' and 'How those flying bugs loved Lucy's white skin!' As the passage continues we become aware of the feelings and thoughts of Harry and, more particularly, Fleury. 'But they could hardly dash forward and seize her with their bare hands. Or could they? Would it be considered permissible in the circumstances?' The saving of Lucy is seen from their point of view. Their knowledge of the female form is solely based on statues and as they shave the insects from Lucy's body they note with 'interest' her pubic hair, as if they were botanists discovering a new flower. Proving problematic, they decide to 'come back to it later'. The drama and comedy of the end is produced by the point of view suddenly switching to the new entrants. We are encouraged to view what Harry and Fleury are doing 'with horror' and, more specifically, to see through the Padre's eyes. He sees several things which mortify him: two men with a naked woman, a damaged Bible and the covers of the Bible being used to 'unclothe' that lady. Fleury's naïvety as he welcomes them 'cheerfully' only adds to the humour.

Farrell is poking fun at Harry and Fleury, but because we are aware of their point of view then that fun is sympathetic. We are meant to enjoy, for example, Fleury getting carried away as if he were sculpting a statue from primeval rock. On the other hand, because the Padre only enters right at the end and because his response is comparatively extreme – all his eyes can see are 'the golden letters "Holy Bible"' – then we are encouraged to view him critically. The whole piece, then, gently mocks the idea of gallant heroes rescuing a lady in distress, heroes who are naïve, ignorant, but well-meaning products of a Victorian society.

Finally

To recap then: in this unit we have been looking at the stance that writers adopt. It might be helpful to think of the *story* as being the facts, the events and *narrative* as being how those facts and events are told. We have been concerned here with narrative and its two main aspects: the relationship of the writer to the story - the point of view - and the relationship of the writer to the reader - the voice. Third-person writing, in its extreme form is purely external; however, because it can so easily reveal a character's feelings and thoughts, it can be very internalized. Or to put it another way, writers can adopt several recognized positions:

◎ the external point of view, which is detached and without insight
◎ the internal point of view, which is pure and sees only what one character sees
◎ the all-seeing, all-knowing omniscient position.

In reality, though, as we have seen, third-person writing can adopt, to a greater or lesser extent, a mixture of these three positions. Further fine tuning can also be seen. The view of the narrator can be *restricted*; this may take two forms. First, the narrator has a limited or self-centred view of things, which may clearly not represent the whole picture: examples of this would be Benjy in Faulkner's *The Sound and the Fury* and Emma in Austen's *Emma*. This may be referred to as the *naïve* narrator. Alternatively, the narrator may choose to appear less dogmatic than the omniscient stance and, in suggesting doubt about the facts of a case, therefore identify more with the position that the reader has. Zahavi does this in the extract from *Dirty Weekend* when she writes '*Perhaps* it was the thought of having been, and gone, and left no mark'.

Extension

1   Collect some more examples of the writing of Hemingway and Carver. Analyse their varying points of view. Present your findings in a seminar.
2   Go back to Austen and find further extracts which reveal internalized thoughts.

Constructing character
1: speech

In the setting up of 'character' in a text, a writer has various decisions to make. We have already seen the importance that the writer's chosen point of view can have in guiding our responses. The internal point of view seems naturally to bring a character's situation closer to the reader through the perspective given and through the amount (and quality) of information given; but, as we have also seen, this isn't always the case. Not all first-person narrators are 'likeable' or honest; and, further, through the use of techniques like free direct thought, even texts written from an external point of view can make us very aware of a character's situation and thinking. These next two units aim to look in more detail at the setting up of 'character' and some of the choices open to writers. First, we will look at some of the implications involved in the representation of speech; the next unit will then concentrate on the choices that writers make in character description.

Speech and dialogue in literature function in various ways. Characters have conversations with each other to enable a third party – the reader – to learn about who they are, what role they are playing and about the events of the novel. Dialogue is, after all, plot-driven. Writers, too, may adopt different speech styles so that we can tell them apart.

A writer's use of speech for a character can obviously be very important to indicate what that character thinks, feels or believes. Speech can be used to suggest personality as well as intelligence, class and education. Speech, too, can be relatively formal, as, for example in many

of the exchanges in Jane Austen's novels; it can operate at the level of caricature, as in the speech of some of the characters in the novels of Dickens; it
can try to be as real or authentic as actual everyday speech. However, the
convention is that, in even the most apparently realistic dialogue, most of
the features of actual speech are tidied up. An examination of a transcript of
actually occurring dialogue should show why this is the case.

Below is an extract from a transcription of an interview with Henry
Cockburn, who played football for Manchester United and England in
the 1940s and 1950s, in which he explains how he first joined the team.
The extract is unpunctuated following the convention of transcribing
spoken language. A full stop in brackets (.) indicates a pause of about half
a second. HC stands for Henry Cockburn, and Int for the interviewer.

Int:	ok how you first came to sign for United because all the books say is er (.) born in Ashton-under-Lyne and then er joined goslings
HC:	that's true
Int:	is there anything to add to that
HC:	no (.) I joined gosling you know and er (.) at that time (.) there was another player playing as well as me that's Jack Compton
Int:	how how what was the age range of the people playing in that
HC:	oh er let's see (.) I should say the average age was about twenty-three
Int:	yeah yeah (.) but you'd have been a bit younger than that wouldn't you
HC:	oh yes I was only about oh whatever (.) nineteenish (.) you know (.) yes
Int:	yeah and what about the actual incident of signing who sort of spotted you
HC:	at that particular time (.) er (.) there's one occasion (.) I was er I had the flu
Int:	yeah
HC:	and one er (.) a man had been round a couple of times a scout for Blackpool (.) and er he wanted me to sign for Blackpool (.) and he came round to sign me (.) one particular (.) Saturday (.) Cyril Edge he was called Mr Edge (.) and his son played for the second team Lancashire second team fast bowler (.) and er (.) I was in bed with the flu and I er he said oh well I'll come again if he's not very well (.) in between that (.) er Bert Whalley who got killed in the cra in the er

Int:	Munich
HC:	Munich air crash
Int:	yeah
HC:	er came along and asked me would I sign for Manchester United (.) amateur forms which I (.) I was quite willing then because it's quite near you see
Int:	yeah
HC:	so that was er (.) that was (.) I says ok yes (.) that was it you know

This transcription is typical of naturally occurring dialogue; it is, though, more tightly structured than natural conversation, being a question and answer format, and, for instance, has fewer interruptions or false starts than might be expected. In conversation we are thinking on our feet and negotiating our turn in a kind of game of verbal tennis and this accounts for the features found here, which are:

- fillers, such as 'er' which allow time to think
- hedges, often 'kind of' or 'sort of', but also forms such as 'you see' and 'you know' which either soften the force with which something is said or get the listener to share in the speaker's view
- reinforcers, which encourage the speaker to continue, as in 'yeah'
- false starts, as in 'how how what was the age range'
- repetition, as in 'so that was er (.) that was'
- the agreement principle, where speakers adopt strategies which include co-operating and agreeing in order to maximize politeness, as in Henry Cockburn's first response of 'that's true'.

Activity

Imagine, now, that the above exchange has been written as if it were to appear in a work of fiction. Consider the differences between the real dialogue and its literary version.

'So, how did you actually come to sign for Manchester United?' the interviewer asked.

'Well,' began Henry, 'I first joined the goslings.'

'How old were the players there?'

Henry shrugged. 'About twenty-three.'

'But,' the interviewer pressed, 'you were younger than that?'

'Yes,' Henry agreed. 'Nineteen.'

'So, anyway, how were you spotted?'

Henry chuckled. 'Well, actually the Blackpool scout, Cyril Edge, came to sign me up one Saturday but I was in bed with flu. He said he'd come back when I was better.'

Then he fell silent.

Eventually he added thoughtfully, 'But in between, the Manchester United scout, Bert Whalley, who got killed in the Munich air crash, asked me to sign for them. And so that's how I ended up with them.'

Commentary

You could play around with this dialogue and add all sorts of extra information. This version, though, tidies up all the repetition of the real conversation, omits the fillers and reinforcers etc. and pares the exchange down to the essential. Notice the extra information given to suggest character: non-verbal forms such as 'shrugged' and prosodic comments to describe how something is said, such as 'he added thoughtfully'.

Class and region

Writers may wish to further suggest character by indicating a character's social class or regional origin. The writing down to suggest a character's accent is largely impressionistic and is a kind of shorthand to signal dialect. It may not be at all phonologically correct. It can only be an approximation. Here is a line from Emily Brontë's *Wuthering Heights*:

> 'Tak' these in tuh t'maister, lad,' he said, 'un' bide theare; aw's gang up tuh my awn rahm.'

Try saying it out loud; does it sound like authentic Yorkshire?

The representation of accent is a simplification of the language in question and is often replicated using a very small number of key features. These features, of course, need to be easily representable in the written form. Some of the features easy to produce on the page are:

- dropping letter(s) at the end of words, e.g. 'nothin'' for 'nothing'
- dropping letter(s) at the beginning of words, e.g. ''orse' for 'horse'
- common, accepted spellings, e.g. 'gotta' for 'got to', 'wanna' for 'want to' and ''cos' for 'because'.

There are some features though, common to many dialects, which are not easy to assimilate into Standard English writing, such as the glottal stop, so these are normally ignored. Just replacing the omitted *ts* in words like 'bottle' or 'butter', for example with the accepted apostrophe mark would not necessarily aid pronunciation. On the page these two words with the glottal stop in place would read like this:

bo'le
bu'er

This attempt to suggest pronunciation - the **phonological** features - by spelling is called **eye dialect**. Writers may use a mixture of phonological features and also **syntactic** features - that is, vocabulary and grammar - to represent a particular dialect.

Activity

The next few extracts all deal with the representation of regional dialect. Answer the various questions, discuss your responses with others, perhaps, and then read the commentary given at the end.

First, read this extract from Thomas Hardy's *Under the Greenwood Tree*. What impression do you get of the character Mail? And why? Be aware of phonological or eye dialect spellings, as in 'feller' as well as grammatical dialect, as in 'knowed'.

'Ay,' said Mail, in a tone of a man who did not agree with everybody as a rule, though he did now; 'I knowed a' auctioneering feller once – a very friendly feller 'a was too. And so one hot day as I was walking down the front street o' Casterbridge, jist below the King's Arms, I passed a' open winder and see him inside, stuck upon his perch, a-selling off. I jist nodded to en in a friendly way as I passed, and went my way, and thought no more about it. Well, next day, as I was oilen my boots by fuel-house door, if a letter didn't come wi' a bill in en, charging me with a feather-bed, bolster, and pillers, that I had bid for at Mr Taylor's sale. The slim-faced martel had knocked 'em down to me because I nodded to en in my friendly way; and I had to pay for 'em too.'

Next, read Mr Knightley's chastisement of Emma (from Jane Austen's *Emma*). He is the gentleman-hero of the book, the only character permitted to talk to the heroine Emma in this way and the one she finally marries at the end of the book. This extract takes place at the end of an excursion to Box Hill where Emma has been rude to Miss Bates.

'Emma, I must once more speak to you as I have been used to do: a privilege rather endured than allowed, perhaps, but I must still use it. I cannot see you acting wrong, without a remonstrance. How could you be so unfeeling to Miss Bates? How could you be so insolent in your wit to a woman of her character, age, and situation? – Emma, I had not thought it possible.'

Now imagine Mr Knightley has a Cockney accent; just a few features have been used. How does your impression of him change?

'Em', I must once more speak to you as I 'ave bin used to do: a privilege rarver endured than allowed, p'raps, but I must still use it. I cannot see you actin' wrong, wivout a remonstrance. 'Ow could you be so unfeelin' to Miss Bates? 'Ow could you be so insolent in your wit to a woman ov 'er character, age, and situation? – Em', I 'ad not fought it possible.'

This last extract is from D. H. Lawrence's *Lady Chatterley's Lover*. Here Lady Chatterley's gamekeeper lover, Mellors, is attempting to teach her his East Midlands dialect. How does your impression of him differ from that of Hardy's Mail?

She lay still. He softly opened the door. The sky was dark blue, with crystalline, turquoise rim. He went out, to shut up the hens, speaking softly to his dog. And she lay and wondered at the wonder of life, and of being.

When he came back she was still lying there, glowing like a gipsy. He sat on the stool by her.

'Tha mun come one naight ter th' cottage, afore tha goos; sholl ter?' he asked, lifting his eyebrows as he looked at her, his hands dangling between his knees.

'Sholl ter?' she echoed, teasing.

He smiled.

'Ay, sholl ter?' he repeated.

'Ay!' she said, imitating the dialect sound.

'Yi!' he said.

'Yi!' she repeated.

'An' slaip wi' me,' he said. 'It needs that. When sholt come?'

'When sholl I?' she said.

'Nay,' he said, 'tha canna do't. When sholt come then?'

''Appen Sunday,' she said.

''Appen a' Sunday! Ay!'

He laughed at her quickly.

'Nay, tha canna,' he protested.

'Why canna I?' she said.

He laughed. Her attempts at the dialect were so ludicrous, somehow.

'Coom then, tha mun goo!' he said.

'Mun I?' she said.

'Maun Ah!' he corrected.

'Why should I say *maun* when you say *mun*?' she protested. 'You're not playing fair.'

Commentary

Hardy's character of Mail probably comes across as an uneducated working-class type; he's open and friendly but rather simple in that he pays for the goods he apparently bid for at auction without any complaint. He's obviously not the stuff that heroes are made from. On the other hand Mr Knightley is altogether a different proposition. Most readers easily assimilate the educated, caring and respected image in which he is represented; certainly, Emma, the heroine of the book, sees him in that light. But what of the Cockney Mr Knightley? Suddenly he now seems uneducated, lazy in speech and certainly not a respected hero for our Emma. The rewrite simply adopts a few characteristics of the Cockney dialect:

◎   dropping of the initial 'h': 'West Ham' becomes 'West 'Am'
◎   'th' is 'f': so 'think' becomes 'fink'
◎   'th' is 'v': so 'father' becomes 'farver'
◎   the tendency to shorten names is adopted: 'Trace' for 'Tracey'.

There is no justification for calling these features 'lazy' or 'imprecise' but, nevertheless, Cockney English does carry the social connotation of an uneducated 'wheeler-dealer' character who is as likely to sell you an imitation Rolex as he is to comment on your rudeness to old ladies when on an excursion to Box Hill.

By contrast, Mellors's East Midlands dialect in the last extract is conveyed as a rich, natural and unpretentious language which reflects his earthiness and his vigour and his love for Lady Chatterley – and which is also a contrast to the sterile and impotent life of Lady Chatterley's husband. Though it's difficult to convey fully what a character stands for or what the writer, in this case Lawrence, wants to say in just one extract, we do get the impression of someone who is proud of his dialect. In the wider context of the novel Mellors's lower-status language is meant to be seen as an apparent contradiction to his life force, his 'natural' intelligence; it is meant to be seen as a rich contrast to the superficial intelligence of the husband which is represented by Standard English. Some dialects are not so stereotyped or so stigmatized; but all have their own rules of grammar, and the final lines of the extract which show Lady Chatterley's confusion over 'mun' and 'maun' neatly illustrate this.

Unless otherwise indicated, it's normally assumed that characters speak in Received Pronunciation, or at least a kind of unmarked 'neutral accent'. But if writers choose to give their characters a strong dialect voice then it's worth pausing to ask why. The conventions of literary writing have established a connection between Standard English and high literary status. Conventionally heroes, and heroines for that matter, speak the Standard English dialect — the 'correct' form of English used in most written texts and taught in schools and the form taught to foreign learners of English. If that is the case, then think of characters from novels who speak in regional dialect — that is, using dialect, or non-standard words and structures, as well as speaking in an accent other than Received Pronunciation. Are they more likely to be servants, fools, villains?

Certainly, traditionally, different speech varieties have been given to characters of a particular type. Think of Cockney lower-class characters in Dickens, rustic superstitious characters in Hardy's novels, servants in Emily Brontë's *Wuthering Heights*. They are all represented as speaking a different variety to Standard English. Some regional dialects, especially in the U.K., carry with them certain connotations and these can't easily be shaken off. Writers may use the impressions that different readers bring to the representation of speech in texts either to confirm stereotypes or perhaps to challenge commonly held assumptions.

Ethnicity

LUTHER   Brumsic Brandon, Jr.

When writers want to indicate a strong black voice they also adopt the same impressionistic description of accent and dialect that is found in the regional representation of speech. There follows an extract from the writing of Walter Mosley which has been seen as quite new - although Alice Walker did this earlier, in *The Color Purple*, for instance - because it features as hero a black detective who apparently speaks in an 'authentic' voice.

Activity

Read this extract from Mosley's *Devil in a Blue Dress*, set in Los Angeles in 1948. The narrator, Easy Rawlins, is talking to Dupree and Coretta; all three are black. How does Mosley attempt to make the conversation authentic? And in what ways is it literary? Consider categorizing different kinds of spelling used, as well as other indications of cohesion between the speakers.

'Miss ya down at the plant, Ease,' Dupree said. 'Yeah, it just ain't the same wit'out you down there t'keep me straight. Them other niggahs just cain't keep up.'

'I guess you have to do without me from now on, Dupree.'

'Uh-uh, no. I cain't live with that. Benny wants you back, Easy. He's sorry he let you go.'

'First I heard of it.'

'You know them I-talians, Ease, they cain't say they sorry 'cause it's a shame to'em. But he wants you back though, I know that.'

'Could we sit down with you and Odell, Easy?' Coretta said sweetly.

'Sure, sure. Get her a chair, Dupree. Com'on pull up here between us, Coretta.'

I called the bartender to send over a quart of bourbon and a pail of chipped ice.

'So he wants me back, huh?' I asked Dupree once we all had a glass.

'Yeah! He told me this very day that if you walked in that door he'd take you back in a minute.'

'First he want me to kiss his be-hind,' I said. I noticed that Coretta's glass was already empty. 'You want me to freshen that, Coretta?'

'Maybe I'll have another lil taste, if you wanna pour.' I could feel her smile all the way down my spine.

Dupree said, 'Shoot, Easy, I told him that you was sorry 'bout what happened an' he's willin' t'let it pass.'

'I'm a sorry man alright. Any man without his paycheck is sorry.'

Dupree's laugh was so loud that he almost knocked poor Odell over with the volume. 'Well see, there you go!' Dupree bellowed. 'You come on down on Friday an' we got yo' job back for sure.'

As part of the suggestion of authentic speech, you might have categorized different kinds of spelling, to indicate phonological features, like this:

◎   words with letter(s) omitted or words run together:
     wit'out
     t'keep
     to'em
     com'on
     'bout
     an'
     willin'
     t'let
     yo'
◎   words written with an accepted abbreviated spelling:
     ya
     uh-uh
     'cause
     huh
     yeah
     wanna
◎   more innovative spelling to suggest either the phonology or the
     stress of a word:
     niggahs
     cain't
     I-talians
     be-hind
     lil

Yet, the dialogue is tightly structured and there is a sense of cohesion. Notice the introduction of 'Benny', who is then referred to as 'he' or 'them I-talians'; there is, also among other links, continual reference to the term 'sorry'. Notice, too, the addition of directions which help suggest action and the way the participants speak – for example, 'Coretta said sweetly' and 'Dupree bellowed'. There is, too, a real sense of social cohesion from the rapid turn-taking and all the naming that is going on. This gives a literary feel to the dialogue, as well as helping to present an affectionate portrayal of black speakers. The sense of group identity is reinforced by the way Dupree stereotypes those outside their immediate group – their Italian boss and 'them other niggahs'.
     The term 'nigger' has traditionally been a derogatory term used by

whites to and about black speakers, particularly dating from the days of slavery. Actually, here, in the Mosley extract, there is something of a derogatory attitude by Dupree to the other black people he's describing, and so the word carries negative connotations – 'them other niggahs' suggests an undifferentiated mass of black workers, slogging on. But, in general, we have to look at who's doing the talking, and whom they're talking to, to decide how a term is being used. Groups who are named negatively can use negative-sounding terms to each other, with a positive meaning of 'we are in the same group'. Terms, however, mean something different when used by people outside that group: so as readers we would have a very different interpretation if it had been a white speaker talking here. The use of 'girls' is a good analogy: a woman can say to a group of her women friends 'come on, girls'; but if a male boss said that to a roomful of female employees, the meaning would be completely different.

Activity

Unlike Mosley's representation of black speech, which employs comparatively few features to mark it off from Standard American English, Mark Twain, in *The Adventures of Huckleberry Finn*, said he wanted to recreate a 'Missouri negro dialect'. In this extract, Jim, a negro slave, is telling Huck's fortune. He has a hair ball which has come from the stomach of an ox and he claims that it talks to him about the future. Reading this extract, what would you say Twain highlights as the main features of a negro dialect? And what impression do you get of Jim?

'Yo' ole father doan' know, yit, what he's a-gwyne to do. Sometimes he spec he'll go 'way, en den agin he spec he'll stay. De bes' way is to res' easy en let de ole man take his own way. Dey's two angels hoverin' roun' 'bout him. One uv 'em is white en shiny, en t'other one is black. De white one gits him to go right, a little while, den de black one sail in en bust it all up. A body can't tell, yit, which one gwyne to fetch him at de las'. But you is all right. You gwyne to have considable trouble in yo' life, en considable joy. Sometimes you gwyne to git hurt, en sometimes you gwyne to git sick; but every time you's gwyne to git well agin. Dey's two gals flyin' 'bout you in yo' life. One uv 'em's light en t'other one is dark. One is rich en t'other is po'. You's gwyne to marry de po' one fust en de rich one by-en-by. You want to keep 'way fum de water as much as you kin, en don't run no resk, 'kase it's down in de bills dat you's gwyne to git hung.'

Some of the main features of Jim's negro dialect that Twain highlights are: firstly, 'r' deletion, especially at the end of words, as in 'yo'' for 'your' and 'po'' for 'poor'. He also indicates 'd' and 't' deletion at the end of words, so that we get 'ole' for 'old', 'en' for 'and', 'bes'' for 'best', 'las'' for 'last'. There is a certain amount of regularizing of vowel sounds, as in 'agin', 'git', 'yit' and 'kin'. We also find 'th' sounds written as 'd', so 'de' for 'the' and 'dey' for 'they'.

Jim's speech certainly marks him out as uneducated but, of course, what he actually says will also convey an impression. He has a simple and superstitious view of life: hair balls talk to him and the future is seen very much in black and white terms. Although Twain has attempted to convey an actual dialect, it could be argued that this kind of representation just creates, or reinforces, a stereotype. It also makes one wonder how far a writer can deviate from the written norm when trying to convey accent and dialect. Bearing in mind the connection between high literary status and Standard English, some writers have deliberately set out to challenge this position by writing in non-standard forms and replicating vernacular speech, warts and all.

Read this opening to Irvine Welsh's *Trainspotting*. The vernacular Edinburgh dialect is not only conveyed in the speech but also in the narrative voice. How difficult is it to read? How much does the way it is written, the use of taboo words and what it is about affect your impressions of the narrator, Rents? Note, there is no commentary.

> The sweat wis lashing oafay Sick Boy; he wis trembling. Ah wis jist sitting thair, focusing oan the telly, tryin no tae notice the cunt. He was bringing me doon. Ah tried tae keep ma attention oan the Jean-Claude Van Damme video.
>
> As happens in such movies, they started oaf wi an obligatory dramatic opening. Then the next phase ay the picture involved building up the tension through introducing the dastardly villain and sticking the weak plot thegither. Any minute now, though, auld Jean-Claude's ready tae git doon tae some serious swedgin.

> - Rents. Ah've goat tae see Mother Superior, Sick Boy gasped, shaking his heid.
>
> - Aw, ah sais. Ah wanted the radge tae jist fuck off ootay ma visage, tae go oan his ain, n jist leave us wi Jean-Claude. Oan the other hand, ah'd be gitting sick tae before long, and if that cunt went n scored, he'd haud oot oan us. They call um Sick Boy, no because he's eywis sick wi junk withdrawal, but because he's just one sick cunt.

Extension

1. Tape and transcribe some real conversations and compare them with authentic-looking dialogue in fiction. Also tape and transcribe scripts from 'realistic' dramas, soap operas, etc. In both cases examine what has been kept in and what has been left out. Film scripts are also readily available and these could form the basis for further investigation.

2. Consider the fact that John Keats was a Cockney, William Wordsworth spoke in a northern accent, so that 'water' rhymed with 'matter', and William Shakespeare came from the Midlands. What questions does that raise for the accents that currently have prestige?

3. Investigate further the challenges presented by texts not written in Standard English. You might look at Irvine Welsh and James Kelman. Iain Banks's *The Bridge* and Iain M. Banks's (the same writer) *Feersum Endjinn* are also worth studying as they both explore the phonetic representation of language.

Constructing character
2: description

Units 2 and 3 took as their focus the broad perspectives of internal and external narrative point of view. Then, in the last unit, constructing character through speech was explored. In practice, though, our ideas or impressions are not compartmentalized: we are aware that characters are more than just how they talk. They are also about how they are seen, what they do and how they behave. This unit will explore how writers describe characters and will use for its focus different presentations of gender.

Activity

Read this extract, which is the opening of Enid Blyton's very first *The Secret Seven* book, published in 1949. What information are we given about Peter and Janet, how are they presented and what do they say?

'We'd better have a meeting of the Secret Seven,' said Peter to Janet. 'We haven't had one for ages.'

'Oh, yes, let's!' said Janet, shutting her book with a bang. 'It isn't that we've forgotten about the Society, Peter - it's just that we've had such a lot of exciting things to do in the Christmas holidays we simply haven't had time to call a meeting.'

'But we must,' said Peter. 'It's no good having a Secret Society unless we use it. We'd better send out messages to the others.'

'Five notes to write,' groaned Janet. 'You're quicker at writing than I am, Peter - you write three and I'll write two.'

'Woof!' said Scamper, the golden spaniel.

'Yes, I know you'd love to write one, too, if you could,' said Janet, patting the silky golden head. 'You can carry one in your mouth to deliver. That can be *your* job, Scamper.'

'What shall we say?' said Peter, pulling a piece of paper towards him and chewing the end of his pen as he tried to think of words.

'Well - we'd better tell them to come here, I think,' said Janet. 'We could use the old shed at the bottom of the garden for a meeting place, couldn't we? Mummy lets us play there in the winter because it's next to the boiler that heats the greenhouse, and it's quite warm.'

'Right,' said Peter, and he began to write. 'I'll do this message first, Janet, and you can copy it. Let's see - we want one for Pam, one for Colin, one for Jack, one for Barbara - who's the seventh of us? I've forgotten.'

'George, of course,' said Janet. 'Pam, Colin, Jack, Barbara, George, you and me - that's the seven - the Secret Seven. It sounds nice, doesn't it?'

The Seven Society was one that Peter and Janet had invented. They thought it was great fun to have a little band of boys and girls who knew the password, and who wore the badge - a button with SS on.

'There you are,' said Peter, passing his sheet of paper to Janet. 'You can copy that.'

'It doesn't have to be my *best* writing, does it?' said Janet. 'I'm so slow if I have to do my best writing.'

'Well - so long as it's readable,' said Peter. 'It hasn't got to go by post.'

Janet read what Peter had written: 'IMPORTANT. A meeting of the Secret Seven will be held tomorrow morning in the shed at the bottom of our garden at 10 o'clock. Please give PASSWORD.'

'Oh, I say - what *was* the last password we had?' said Janet in alarm. 'It's so long since we had a meeting that I've forgotten.'

'Well, it's a good thing for you that you've got me to remind you,' said Peter. 'Our latest password is Wenceslas, because we wanted a Christmassy one. Fancy you forgetting that!'

'Oh, yes, of course. Good King Wenceslas,' said Janet. 'Oh, dear - now I've gone and made a mistake in this note already. I really mustn't talk while I'm doing it.'

There was a silence as the two of them wrote their notes. Janet always wrote with her tongue out, which made her look very funny. But she said she couldn't write properly unless her tongue *was* out, so out it had to come.

Commentary

Gender stereotyping – that is, portraying boys/men and girls/women in a narrow, generalized and fixed way – can start at an early age. Much of the traditional literature written for children from the 1940s onwards set out clearly differentiated roles for boys and girls. Typical learner-reader books would feature more male characters than females, and these male characters would take part in a wider range of activities. And this was not only applied to boys and girls, male and female adults, too, had their given place. A typical story might feature the girl helping her mother to make the beds, shop and then cook the evening meal for the husband/ father who invariably did some highly important job as a scientist. After dinner, while the women washed up, the son might help his father with a more masculine-type job like washing the car. And, of course, if there were more dangerous jobs to do, like saving cats from trees, or even thwarting unscrupulous villains, then it had to be for the boys to do. This opening from *The Secret Seven* gives some idea of the different roles meted out to boys and girls.

Peter clearly is in control; he instigates the action to call a meeting of the Secret Seven. On the other hand Janet's role is very much as one of support; she comments on how much quicker Peter is at writing, for example. She's given the job of copying Peter's note, yet she's slow at writing, can't talk and write at the same time and is pictured as looking funny with her tongue out. Her speech is full of 'oh yes' and 'oh I say'; she 'groans' and she speaks in 'alarm'. Peter, however, gives the orders and, even when he admits to having forgotten the seventh member, Janet simply informs him. But when *she* admits to having forgotten the password, Peter talks to her in a patronizing way, like a father to a child: 'Well, it's a good thing for you that you've got me to remind you . . . Fancy you forgetting that!'

Activity

In the adult world of Sir Arthur Conan Doyle's Sherlock Holmes stories, men and women, too, acted out their largely differentiated roles. Read this extract from near the opening of *The Speckled Band*. What information are we given about Sherlock Holmes and the woman who arrives unexpectedly? From the way they are described what impression do you get of them?

> It was early in April, in the year '83, that I woke one morning to find Sherlock Holmes standing fully dressed, by the side of my bed. He was a late riser as a rule, and, as the clock on the mantelpiece showed me that it was only a quarter past seven, I blinked up at him in some surprise, and perhaps just a little resentment, for I was myself regular in my habits.
>
> 'Very sorry to knock you up, Watson,' said he, 'but it's the common lot this morning. Mrs Hudson has been knocked up, she retorted upon me, and I on you.'
>
> 'What is it, then? A fire?'
>
> 'No, a client. It seems that a young lady has arrived in a considerable state of excitement, who insists upon seeing me. She is waiting now in the sitting-room. Now, when young ladies wander about the Metropolis at this hour of the morning, and knock sleepy people up out of their beds, I presume that it is something very pressing which they have to communicate. Should it prove to be an interesting case, you would, I am sure, wish to follow it from the outset. I thought at any rate that I should call you, and give you the chance.'

'My dear fellow, I would not miss it for anything.' I had no keener pleasure than in following Holmes in his professional investigations, and in admiring the rapid deductions, as swift as intuitions, and yet always founded on a logical basis, with which he unravelled the problems which were submitted to him. I rapidly threw on my clothes, and was ready in a few minutes to accompany my friend down to the sitting-room. A lady dressed in black and heavily veiled, who had been sitting in the window, rose as we entered.

'Good morning, madam,' said Holmes cheerily. 'My name is Sherlock Holmes. This is my intimate friend and associate, Dr. Watson, before whom you can speak freely as before myself. Ha, I am glad to see that Mrs Hudson has had the good sense to light the fire. Pray draw up to it, and I shall order you a cup of hot coffee, for I observe that you are shivering.'

'It is not cold which makes me shiver,' said the woman in a low voice, changing her seat as requested.

'What then?'

'It is fear, Mr Holmes. It is terror.' She raised her veil as she spoke, and we could see that she was indeed in a pitiable state of agitation, her face all drawn and grey, with restless, frightened eyes, like those of some hunted animal. Her features and figure were those of a woman of thirty, but her hair was shot with premature grey, and her expression was weary and haggard. Sherlock Holmes ran her over with one of his quick, all-comprehensive glances.

'You must not fear,' said he soothingly, bending forward and patting her forearm. 'We shall soon set matters right, I have no doubt. You have come in by train this morning, I see.'

'You know me, then?'

'No, but I observe the second half of a return ticket in the palm of your left glove. You must have started early, and yet you had a good drive in a dog-cart, along heavy roads, before you reached the station.'

The lady gave a violent start, and stared in bewilderment at my companion.

'There is no mystery, my dear madam,' said he, smiling. 'The left arm of your jacket is pattered with mud in no less than seven places. The marks are perfectly fresh. There is no vehicle save a dog-cart which throws up mud in that way, and then only when you sit on the left-hand side of the driver.'

Commentary

The incident is recounted by Dr Watson, who is in evident awe of his friend's abilities. Holmes's whole attitude towards the lady is patronizing. He comments: 'when young ladies wander about the Metropolis at this hour of the morning, and knock sleepy people up out of their beds, I presume that it is something very pressing which they have to communicate'.

She is presented very much as a damsel in distress: in a 'pitiable state of agitation ... with frightened eyes, like those of some hunted animal'. In direct contrast, the 'hero' Sherlock Holmes is all-seeing and all-knowing – running 'her over with one of his quick, all-comprehensive glances'. He comforts the woman – speaking 'soothingly, bending forward and patting her forearm' and then astounds her – and probably Dr Watson too – with a detailed account, based solely on observation, of how she travelled that morning. 'Knocking you up' by the way, here, means *waking* you up.

Activity

These next two extracts are first-person narratives from two more private eyes. Consider the gender of the narrators. What impressions do you get of them?

Extract 1

I put on a pair of clean jeans and a T-shirt and wandered out to the kitchen. A depressing sight - pans stacked around the sink, crumbs on the table, an old piece of aluminium foil, cheese congealed on the stove from a pasta primavera I'd made a few nights ago. I set about washing up - there are days when the mess hits you so squarely that you can't add to it.

The refrigerator didn't have much of interest in it. The wooden clock by the back door said nine - too late to go out for dinner, as tired as I was, so I settled for a bowl of canned pea soup and some toast.

> *Extract 2*
>
> It was about eleven o'clock in the morning, mid October, with the sun not shining and a look of hard wet rain in the clearness of the foothills. I was wearing my powder-blue suit, with dark blue shirt, tie and display handkerchief, black brogues, black wool socks with dark blue clocks on them. I was neat, clean and sober, and I didn't care who knew it. I was everything the well-dressed private detective ought to be. I was calling on four million dollars.

Commentary

The first extract presents us with the minutiae and reality of domestic life. It seems odd for a man to be concerned with the mess in his kitchen. The description of the mess is also strangely detailed and very tangible – 'cheese congealed on the stove' – and the narrator is precise about what was made a few nights before – 'a pasta primavera'. And would a 'real man' settle 'for a bowl of canned pea soup and some toast' thinking nine o'clock too late to go out for dinner? On the other hand, the narrator in the second extract conveys pride in appearance and aggression in being 'neat, clean and sober' and 'didn't care who knew it'. Also, does the mention of being sober suggest that the female narrator is an alcoholic? And do women ever mention their socks?

The first extract is actually from *Deadlock* by Sara Paretsky, and it features her female detective V. I. Warshawski; the second extract is the opening to Raymond Chandler's *The Big Sleep* and in it the private eye Philip Marlowe describes how he looks and feels. Writing some fifty years after Chandler, Paretsky writes in the same tradition: the lone and lonely investigator, working unsociable hours with kitchens (and sometimes bedrooms) in squalor.

Activity

This next extract is also written very much in the Raymond Chandler tradition. What gender do you think the private eye narrator is and why? How does this text fit in with traditional expectations of the genre?

Any doubts about taking on the case disappeared as soon as I saw and spoke to Sonia Deerfield. I'd always been a sucker for redheads; and Sonia's head blazed with thick, long, copper-red hair the colour of an Irish setter's. That alone wouldn't have been enough to make me take notice. She also had a quality of repressed tension which spoke volumes about the stress she was under and the control she had to exercise over herself just to function. Her control was perfect, much too perfect. She felt vulnerable and no amount of control could quite hide it. Certainly, if she wanted my help she could have it.

Commentary

The extract about Sonia Deerfield is from *Bayou City Secrets* by Deborah Powell, and features a lesbian detective. She writes with affectionate parody of Chandler's 'hard-boiled' style. In Chandler's genre of detective fiction women spell trouble, and of one female villain Marlowe says 'she was slim, dark and lovely and smiling. Reeking with sex. Utterly beyond the moral laws of this or any world I could imagine.' Powell, though, turns traditional expectations on their heads; gone is the male sleuth and the damsel in distress. In its place is a world where female detectives can give us delicious descriptions of damsels who certainly aren't in distress, and which are all the more provocative for being unexpected.

Activity

In the more conservative world of popular romantic fiction, often given the shorthand name 'Mills and Boon' after the principal British publishers of this genre, physical descriptions are also very important, as well as explicit descriptions of feelings. How would you describe the representation of the woman in this extract? Also rewrite the passage, changing the gender words as appropriate, for example:

> He stretched, then, arching his body toward the warmth of the sun, and her breath caught. Gone was the girlish fourteen-year-old's figure she remembered ...

What effect have you created?

> She stretched, then, arching her body toward the warmth of the sun, and his breath caught. Gone was the boyish fourteen-year-old's figure he remembered. Lush womanly curves strained the thin fabric of her T-shirt and denim shorts. He felt a shaft of desire flash through him as he stared, transfixed. Fourteen years had made a hell of a difference in Frank Castillo's daughter. Although, she'd always been a captivating little waif, with those big, doe-soft eyes of hers. Bambi eyes. Their startling greenish-brown color could ensnare a man in an instant. And there'd been her full, slightly pouting mouth.
>
> Dawn Carroll, *Beguiled*

Commentary

Here we have woman as desired object and seen (and felt) very much from the man's point of view. The reader is placed in a voyeuristic position, and this is perhaps not surprising as the man is viewing Frank Castillo's daughter through binoculars. She is described sensually with animal-like detail: 'doe-soft ... Bambi eyes', with the idea of being meek and vulnerable; yet she can 'captivate' and 'ensnare'. Note, too, the clichéd 'short cut' language of 'shaft of desire' and 'full, slightly pouting mouth'. In fact writing like this uses **collocations**, words which commonly go together. Mouths always pout, curves are lush, eyes are doe-soft. Has changing the gender of the participants here disturbed the conventions of this kind of writing? Collect other examples from Mills and Boon, or similar, writing and do a similar job of changing the gender words. Do you become aware of any patterns in the words given to males and females? How differently do the two sexes act?

Activity

Compare these next two extracts. How do they differ in their presentation of the central female character? Both are third-person narrative writing but one adopts a much more internalized point of view.

Extract 1

A smothered grumbling. Sally withdrew her head from the thin coverings and yawned. Eighteen, a gorgeous creature whose native beauty her shabbiness could not hide. Eyes dark, lustrous, haunting; abundant black hair tumbling in waves; a full, ripe, pouting mouth and a low, round bosom. A face and form such as any society dame would have given three-quarters of her fortune to possess. Sally wore it carelessly as though youth's brief hour was eternal; as though there was no such thing as old age. She failed in her temper; but when roused, colour tinted her pallid cheeks such as the wind whipped up when it blew from the north or east.

(Walter Greenwood, *Love on the Dole*)

Extract 2

Helen looks into the mirror. She sees her own face, familiar and yet sharpened up, focused, by her expression of eagerness and anxiety. In a moment she will be utterly changed. She will have holes in her ears. She will have acted upon her own body, and altered it.

   – All right, she says.

   The pain is bearable, lasting only a second. Helen looks at herself in the mirror again. Same green eyes, same curly hair, same broad nose. But in one ear she has a gold stud, and in the other a diamante one. She begins to smile, and then to laugh, and jumps off the couch to parade for Beth, who smiles back at her and then begins to laugh at Helen's smug expression ...

   She walks down the street as proud as a queen, holding her head high, her hair tucked well behind her ears so that her new studs show, balancing her head delicately on her neck, her head with its two new weights, its decoration. She hears the rev of car engines, she looks at adverts for vodka and hair-spray, she wants to babble of red parrots screaming in a green shade. And all the time she buys ice-cream and chatters to Beth and laughs with her as they try on old clothes at the stalls, she catches glimpses, out of the corner of her eye, of decorated female bodies that flash like fish in blue and green pools, that float like birds under blue and green suns, and is rendered speechless.

Michèle Roberts, *The Visitation*

The first extract is very much like the Carroll extract. We get an external description of Sally which stresses her beauty in sensual and animal-like imagery. We are made to notice her 'smothered grumbling' and 'yawn' as she emerges from the 'thin coverings'. Modifiers are heaped around the head nouns to create the effect of abundance and depth:

pre-modifiers	head noun	post-modifiers
eighteen, a gorgeous	creature	
	eyes	dark, lustrous, haunting
abundant black	hair	tumbling in waves
a full, ripe, pouting	mouth	
a low, round	bosom	

Colour, too, is abundant, imagery is extended – 'wind/whipped up/blew' – and Sally's age is also considered important. Notice, also, the collocations of 'low, round bosom' and 'full, ripe, pouting mouth' which is reminiscent of the Carroll text.

The second extract is much more sensitive; we get an internal view of Helen's feelings. We are made aware of her point of view, we see through her eyes as she 'looks into the mirror ... sees her own face, familiar and yet sharpened up, focused, by her expression of eagerness and anxiety'. We feel/sense the momentary pain of the ear-piercing, share her pleasure at her transformation and understand her walking 'down the street as proud as a queen'. There is less emphasis here on her physical appearance and more on her feelings. The focus is sensuous rather than sensual: we hear what she hears, see what she sees. This means, then, that we share her wonder and excitement and, as such, this adopts a similar stance to the Angela Carter extract from *The Magic Toyshop*, given in Unit 1.

1 Compare original texts with their newer editions. You could, for example, look at some of Enid Blyton's original stories which have been re-written to take account of criticisms about stereotyping. Here is an example of a change, relating to gender, from the first *The Secret Seven* (1949). Well into their adventure one of the girls asks a question:

> 'Can't we girls come too?' asked Pam.
>
>   'I don't want to!' said Barbara.
>
>   'Well, you can't come, anyhow,' said Peter. 'That's absolutely certain. Boys only are in the performance to-night!'

And later we find this:

> 'I've thought of something,' said Jack at last. 'It's a bit frightening, though. We couldn't let the girls into it.'
>
>   'Whatever is it?' said all three girls at once.

However, by 1992 we find a revised version of the story and the two extracts given above now read like this:

> 'Can't we girls come too?' asked Pam.
>
>   'I don't want to!' said Barbara.
>
>   'No,' said Peter. 'I am sorry but seven is too many. We'll have more chance of success if there are only four of us.'
>
>   'I've thought of something,' said Jack at last. 'It's a bit frightening, though.'
>
>   'Whatever is it?' chorused the others.

2   Sherlock Holmes is one of a type of intelligent, principled heroes in whom we can have absolute faith and trust. Another type is Miss Marple, Agatha Christie's amateur sleuth: a well-meaning spinster with time on her hands and no obvious domestic or money problems, solving mysteries in amongst the jumble sales and tea and scones of genteel England. But if you were to think of a hero or

heroine now, then who would you name? Collect examples of other heroes or heroines. How are they portrayed? A starting point might be to consider current television programmes, such as police dramas or hospital series.

3   Consider the presentation of characters in gay and lesbian writing, and writing that challenges ideas about sexuality. You might try:

◎   *Desert of the Heart* by Jane Rule, which is a lesbian love story, now made into a film, called *Desert Hearts*

◎   *Herland* by Charlotte Perkins Gilman, which is about an all-female community where women live in peace and harmony, until disturbed by three male explorers

◎   *Woman on the Edge of Time* by Marge Piercy, where in her fantasy world gender doesn't exist

◎   *Putting the Boot In* by Dan Kavanagh, which concerns the adventures of bisexual private eye Duffy.

4   Pick a theme or an experience and look at it from a gender point of view, for example a sexual encounter. You might try comparing accounts from D. H. Lawrence's *Lady Chatterley's Lover* with relevant descriptions in Michèle Roberts's *The Visitation*.

Pop fiction

The brief introduction in the previous unit to the style of writing often referred to as the 'Mills and Boon' style, which helped illustrate how gender roles can be portrayed, probably confirmed the traits which we instinctively recognize. But what are these traits? Can we analyse the formulaic pattern these stories employ? This unit will attempt to high-light some of the more obvious kinds of language that writers of popular romance fiction use. This is not just work published by Mills and Boon – publishing houses like Silhouette, for instance, issue work of this type; the genre of writing we are concerned with is as easily found in magazines and on the racks at rail stations and airports.

The unit will begin with an examination of the lexis typically used in these books and then go on to consider some of the syntactic features also found. Having drawn attention to these features, the unit ends with a complete short story fairly typical of the genre.

The lexis

One key feature in pop fiction is the kind of reporting word used to describe dialogue. Characters rarely 'say'; instead they 'murmur', 'grunt', 'agree'; moreover they often 'murmur seductively', 'grunt tersely', 'agree readily'. This short extract is fairly typical:

'I am so sorry to have startled you,' Carlo Saracini purred, lying between his even white teeth.

Her own teeth clenched. She wanted to reach down the telephone line and slap him stupid. And feeling that way again ... feeling that alien surge of raw violent hatred which he alone invoked ... scared her rigid. Her mouth went dry. 'What do you want?'

'I'm in a very generous mood,' he imparted with a husky edge to his slow slightly accented drawl. 'I'm prepared to offer you a meeting –'

Her fingers clenched like talons round the receiver. 'A meeting ... why?'

'Can it be that you haven't seen your father yet?' he murmured.

She went white. 'I've seen him,' she whispered, not troubling to add that Gerald Amory was still in the room next door.

'Embezzlement is a very serious offence.'

'He had gambling debts,' Jessica protested in a feverish undertone. 'He panicked ... he didn't mean to take the money from the firm! He was borrowing it –'

'Euphemistically speaking,' Carlo inserted with more than an edge of mockery.

'Amory's used to belong to him,' Jessica reminded him with helpless bitterness.

'But it doesn't now,' Carlo traded softly. 'Now it belongs to me.'

(Lynne Graham, *The Heat of Passion*)

A word like 'say' is **unmarked**, that is, it is a neutral word and carries no particular connotations. Also referred to as core vocabulary (see Carter 1987), these unmarked words are often replaced with synonyms in pop fiction. Using reporting words like 'purr' or 'murmur' pack the language with extra sensation and give the impression of busy and ready-to-act characters. And if the reporting words still seem lacking, then extra adjectival phrases are employed to add further emphasis, as in:

> he imparted *with a husky edge to his slow slightly accented drawl*
> Jessica protested *in a feverish undertone*
> Carlo inserted *with more than an edge of mockery*
> Jessica reminded him *with helpless bitterness*

And sometimes, in the effort to avoid using an unmarked word, words which are almost meaningless in context are employed, as in 'Carlo traded softly'.

In *The Heat of Passion*, from which the above dialogue is taken, there follow two paragraphs of background information – which are examined later in the unit. In this extract the dialogue then continues but all the reporting words have been replaced by 'said' and the omitted words given here. Decide where the missing words belong.

blurted in desperation
enquired gently
specified
gasped
mused provocatively
seethed down the phone in outrage
breathed reflectively

'Dad intended to repay the money ... if it hadn't have been for the audit, you wouldn't even have found out!' she *said*.

'Why do you think I spring occasional surprise audits on my companies?' Carlo *said*. 'Employees like your father get greedy and sometimes they get caught as he has with their hands trapped in the till.'

Jessica trembled, her heartbeat thundering deafeningly in her eardrums. His deliberate cruelty appalled her. 'He wasn't greedy ... he was desperate!'

'I'm willing to meet you to-night. I'm staying at the Deangate Hall. I'm sure I don't need to tell you which suite I'll be occupying. Eight,' he *said*. 'I will wait one minute past the hour, no more. If you're not there, there'll be no second chance.'

Aghast at the site he had specified and absolutely enraged by his instinctive sadism, Jessica *said*, 'Don't waste your time! I'll see you in hell before I set foot inside that hotel again!'

'You must have been quite a sight limping out on one shoe that afternoon,' Carlo *said*. 'The chambermaid found the other one under the bed. I still have it. Cinderella's slipper –'

'How dare you?' she *said*.

'And as I recall it, you damned near left something far more intimate behind,' Carlo *said*.

Commentary

The omitted words belong in the same order as in the list, so that the extract should read:

> 'Dad intended to repay the money ... if it hadn't have been for the audit, you wouldn't even have found out!' she *blurted in desperation.* 'Why do you think I spring occasional surprise audits on my companies?' Carlo *enquired gently.'*

and so on. But, interestingly, some of the terms could be interchanged without any difference in reading – which highlights their purely functional nature. They push the dialogue along and are also a constant reminder of who is actually speaking.

Kath chuckled, Ben grinned

Another feature of some of the marked reporting words used in pop fiction is the use of the added manner adverb. Adverbs are added, again, in an attempt to heighten emphasis, though they are often redundant or even nonsensical. Forms, then, like 'he grunted tersely' are employed where 'tersely' is largely redundant; grunting is, after all, naturally terse - it would be hard to imagine a *protracted* grunt; similarly, 'she whispered quietly'. On the other hand, forms like 'he breathed reflectively' or 'she muttered stiffly' don't really make much sense at all. Sometimes some variety is achieved by forms indicating physical response such as: 'chuckled', 'grinned', 'shrugged' or whatever. We could find, then, something like this:

> 'I think he likes you.'
> Kath chuckled. 'Do you think so?'
> 'Yes I do,' Ben grinned back.

Again, unmarked forms - in this case 'laughed' and 'smiled' - are considered too plain and unadventurous.

The two other word classes which are often used in a marked form are verbs and adjectives. Collect some examples from pop fiction. How often can the verbs and adjectives be rewritten in a more unmarked, neutral form? Do characters 'hurry', rush', 'speed' rather than 'walk'? Do they 'look' or do they 'shoot furious glances'? Are they 'skinny' or 'slim' rather than the unmarked 'thin'? Are their eyes 'blue' or 'smoky turquoise'?

The general effect, then, of using marked forms of vocabulary is one of busy, exciting, larger-than-life characters. They are engaged in dialogue, chuckling and grinning at each other; and they don't just 'glance' or even 'shoot glances' but 'shoot furious glances'.

Descriptions of bodies

Physical descriptions are very important in pop fiction, and none more so than the appearances of the heroine and hero. Take a few moments to jot down how they might be described.

Activity

Compare these two extracts. What impression are we meant to get? Do you note any similarities in the language used?

Extract 1

The face surrounded by the soft blonde hair was somewhat wide with a strong jawline, but its individual features were classical, clean cut, well defined - high cheekbones, straight nose, pretty mouth, chin that was firm and resolute without being pugnacious. The eyes, set wide apart under arched blonde brows, were large and clear, their colour a light sea-blue that was almost but not quite turquoise. The features came together to create a face that was unusually attractive, lively with vivid intelligence and humour, highly photogenic. In her bare feet, as she was now, she stood five feet six inches tall; slender of frame yet surprisingly strong, she had long legs and possessed a willowy grace.

Extract 2

She studied the dark planes of his impassive features, the clear golden eyes set beneath winged black brows and the savagely high cheekbones which lent such fierce strength to his face. Her face glossed over the stubborn jut of a decidedly Greek nose and the wide perfection of his narrow mouth before hurriedly falling away.

Commentary

Extract 1 describes the heroine of Barbara Taylor Bradford's *Remember* and extract 2 describes the villain in Lynne Graham's Mills and Boon romance *The Heat of Passion*. Perhaps surprisingly, the two portraits share some features:

Her	Him
strong, firm, resolute	strength
eyes set under arched brows	eyes set beneath winged brows
(with colour)	(with colour)
eyes: clear + colour	eyes: clear + colour
classical	Greek
high cheekbones	high cheekbones

Certain facial features, then, seem to be desirable regardless of sex or personality. But with the addition of stock adjectives the heroine and the villain are drawn in two different lights. So that we read:

Her	Him
soft	impassive
pretty	savagely
attractive	fierce
grace	stubborn

Although these two descriptions do share features, it's fairly clear which one is meant to get our approval.

Of course some texts set out to be more explicit than others; the target audience, too, may be quite narrowly defined. In these cases it seems reasonable to expect that the more explicit the text or the more clearly defined the audience is, then the more explicit or targeted the language.

Activity

Here are five descriptions of men. Match them to these five writers/ sources:

Michèle Roberts
Barbara Taylor Bradford
Jackie Collins

Caroline Anderson ('Mills and Boon')
Judi Hughes (*more!,* a teenage magazine)

You may need to do a little research first. (An extract from Michèle Roberts appears in Unit 5.)

Extract 1

Jack Python walked through the lobby of the Beverly Hills Hotel with every eye upon him. He had money, charisma, a certain kind of power, razor-sharp wit and fame. It all showed. He was six feet tall with virile good looks. Thick black hair worn just a tad too long, penetrating green eyes, a two-day stubble on a deep suntan, and a hard body. He was thirty-nine years old and he had the world by the balls.

Extract 2

His dark, lively eyes are closed, the lashes swept down, and his bony features are relaxed in sleep, his mouth gentle. Black hairs, very fine, grow thickly on his chest, as satiny as grass, tapering, beneath his collar-bone, to the flick of a paintbrush loaded with one full, heavy drop of black.

Extract 3

I'll never forget the first time I saw him. Luiz was sitting at one of the beach tables with a small, dark-haired girl. He looked so delicious, with soft black curly hair and a strong, toned body that shone deep brown in the sun. It was the girl who approached me, smiling.

'My brother wants to buy you a drink,' she said.

Brother! Yes! I glowed with relief.

'So why doesn't he ask me himself then?'

'He doesn't speak any English,' she explained. 'Well? Would you like to join us?'

'There doesn't seem much point if he . . .'

And that was when I looked across at him and he smiled that slow, sexy smile, and it didn't seem to matter that we couldn't communicate. I just wanted to be near him.

Extract 4

Perhaps it was his smile, the hesitant, slightly quirky twist to his lips, gone as swiftly as it had come; or perhaps the eyes, that strange combination of ice-blue and the dark, practically navy line around the iris that gave them a penetrating, almost haunting quality. Whatever it was, Helen Cooper found his presence at the meeting distracting in the extreme.

Extract 5

Clee did not have the glamorous movie-star looks she had expected him to have, although he was quite good looking in a clean cut, all-American way. He had a *nice* face, that was the best way of describing it, and it was one that was open and honest. His hair was dark, his eyes brown, their expression gentle, and his sensitive mouth was quick to smile. He was about five feet ten inches in height, but appeared to be taller since his body was lean and athletic.

Commentary

The extracts are from:

1 Jackie Collins
2 Michèle Roberts
3 Judi Hughes
4 Caroline Anderson
5 Barbara Taylor Bradford

Jackie Collins's books – this extract is the opening of *Hollywood Husbands* – are sometimes referred to as 'bonkbusters' for reasons which are probably obvious even from the few lines given here. The other writers, or sources, are all worth following up. Ask yourself how far the features we are concerned with here become more or less prominent according to the status of the writer. Also, can any gradation be found in magazines aimed at different audiences? Extract 3 has come from an erotic story in *more!* magazine. How do the stories compare in magazines such as *Woman* or *Cosmopolitan* for example? This whole area is rich for potential study.

As far as the descriptions of heroines themselves are concerned we find that they typically view themselves in the mirror; otherwise we wouldn't know what they looked like, as in this passage discussed by Nash (1990):

> She had been in and out of the pool all day and her bathing suit was hanging from the shower tap. Before reaching for it, she paused for a moment to look at herself in the full-length mirror. A tall girl with sun-streaked blonde hair, long brown legs and a curvy figure which she would have liked to be slimmer but which she wasn't displeased with.

It would be stylistically out of place for the writer to intervene and comment that the heroine was good-looking, if a little on the large side; events are generally viewed from the point of view of the heroine, including how she herself looks to her.

The extended metaphor

In describing bodies we find that eyes, the mouth – lips, smile, teeth – and hair are normally key features; but never the ears. Height and body build also figure: men need to be at least six feet tall, women about six to eight inches shorter and both must be slim, with the man muscular but never a body-builder. Eyes come in all shades of colour – but never just blue – and they are often described in terms of their light intensity. We find, therefore:

her eyes glowed brilliantly
his eyes beamed brightly
burnished golden eyes
blazing violet eyes
her eyes glittered like brilliant amethysts.

Pop fiction has a tendency to use these **extended metaphors** or to say the same thing in several ways. This is done to add emphasis and to give the impression of more action, more pain, or whatever. The result, though, may be over-emphasis rather than amplification; not enlightenment but just more of the same, which may prove to be nonsensical. Some examples of over-emphasis taken from the opening pages of *The Heat of Passion* are:

slow drawl
raw violent
thundering deafeningly
lively and vivid
absolutely enraged
terrifyingly loyal
immense vacuum
highly photogenic

To make the point: 'photogenic' is an absolute term meaning very attractive in photographs or on camera; being 'highly ...' doesn't really make sense. Similarly, being 'enraged' should be sufficient; 'absolutely' really adds nothing and, if anything, detracts from the power of 'enraged'.

Other examples from the same pages include: 'guilt stabbed like a knife into Jessica' – where the use of 'stabbed' makes 'like a knife' redundant; 'scorching heat surged through her shivering body in an unstoppable surge' – really too much surging here; and 'nausea stirred in her stomach, churned up by a current of raw loathing so powerful, she could taste it' – just imagine all that stirring and churning.

Women at the mercy of their bodies

Another common feature of pop fiction is the passive way women are represented, especially those in love. As subjects in clause constructions they often do not actually *act* upon anything or anybody: they 'feel faint/aglow/content' rather than 'feel him' for instance. As such, women as subjects are used with verbs in an *intransitive* mode: they 'love', they 'suffer', they 'tremble'. When copular or 'linking' verbs are employed then the construction follows SVC, where S = subject, V = verb and C = complement. Some forms would be:

she was ecstatic
she felt faint
she grew weary
she turned cold
she stayed silent.

These verbs 'link' because they are able to link the complement meaning with the subject, tell us more about the subject.

Furthermore, women are often not the **agent** in constructions but are acted upon, even to the extent that their own body, or parts of it, seem to have lives of their own or, certainly, more power than the woman herself. So instead of finding 'she cried', where 'she' is the agent, that is, she is actually doing the act of crying, we find something like 'tears sprang to her eyes', where the 'tears' are doing the action and the woman is at their mercy. Constructions like this also often go hand in hand with marked verbs. So tears 'spring/flow/gush'; tears can 'tighten the throat'. Here are some examples, almost taken at random:

her teeth clenched
heat crawled up her slender throat
a choked laugh that was no laugh at all escaped her
her gaze fell on the table exquisitely set for two
her smooth brow furrowed.

In the attempt to achieve effect, however, the result can be almost comic, as in the image of heat 'crawling' up a slender throat. Sometimes, however, even the man finds parts of *his* body taking control. On the same few pages that the examples above come from we find this:

> Carlo cast the phone aside and crossed the room in a couple of long strides. Confident hands undid the sash at her waist, parted her coat and slid it off her tense shoulders as if she were a doll to be undressed.

Particularly when stories reach passionate moments, then the hands become the agents and take over. Some final examples from Carlo and Jessica:

> Her *hands* fluttered over every part of him ... her *nails* skidded down the long sweep of his back ... rawly impatient *hands* dealt with the scrap of silk that was all that shielded her from him. 'You're mine from this moment on,' Carlo spelt out roughly, 'you are mine.'

Doing it in twos

As well as certain key lexical constructions in pop fiction, which tell us which genre we are reading, there is a syntactic feature which is also common. This is a construction which gives the impression, again, of activity. Heroines and heroes always seem to be doing at least two things at once. Walter Nash in his *Language in Popular Fiction* (1990) details various grammatical constructions and this is worth reading for further exploration. A typical construction is:

> Squaring her shoulders, she pressed the doorbell with a resolute finger.

The main action here is the pressing of the doorbell with a resolute finger. The secondary action is the squaring of the shoulders. Grammatically, 'she pressed the doorbell with a resolute finger' is the main clause, and 'squaring her shoulders' is a dependent clause. It cannot stand alone, whereas 'she pressed the doorbell with a resolute finger' can. More strictly speaking, 'squaring her shoulders' is called a **present participle clause**. In cases like this present participle clauses describe the 'manner' of action or behaviour. Here are three examples, in just one paragraph, from the second page of Bradford's *Remember*.

> *Pushing herself up against the pillows*, she switched on the bedside lamp, glanced at her watch. It was a few minutes before ten. *Throwing back the covers decisively*, she got out of bed and hurried across the floor to the window. *Opening it wide*, she stepped out onto the balcony, anxious to see what, if anything, was happening in the streets of Beijing.

If the various actions are examined, however, they might be found to be incompatible. For example, squaring your shoulders as you press a doorbell resolutely is actually not that easy. Also pushing yourself up against a pillow, switching on the bedside lamp and glancing at your watch more or less simultaneously takes some doing. Another interesting feature of this construction is that sometimes the apparent order of the actions can be altered without affecting the meaning. So we could write, for example:

Pressing the doorbell with a resolute finger, she squared her shoulders.
Switching on the bedside lamp, she glanced at her watch, pushed herself up against the pillows.

Other constructions which can be found, though less frequently, are the use of the **past participle clause** before the main clause. Even more so than the present participle clause, the positioning of the past participle clause at the start of the sentence helps focus attention on the subject. For example:

Incensed by his comment, Kath slammed down the phone.
Awakened by the noise, Ben threw back the covers.
Alerted to his concerns, Angie spoke soothingly.

Reverse the order of the clauses in these three examples. Is there a shift of focus? For example:

Kath slammed down the phone, incensed by his comment.

Activity

Collect further examples from your own reading. How interchangeable is the syntactic order of clauses? Do some of your own writing where you push to the extreme the frequency of such constructions. Also do some rewriting of your own examples, and ones you have collected, where you reduce the number of participle clauses. What effects are created? Here is a simple rewrite of the Bradford paragraph. How does it now read?

I pushed myself up against the pillows, switched on the bedside lamp and glanced at my watch. It was a few minutes before ten. I threw back the covers and got out of bed and hurried across the floor to the window. I opened it wide. I stepped out onto the balcony, anxious to see what, if anything, was happening in the streets of Beijing.

The recaps, the questions and the moralizing

There are three final features of pop fiction worth noticing. Openings tend to grab the reader's attention with descriptions of heroines or heroes, or with clear accounts of how character A views/thinks about/is trying to forget, etc., character B. Having established some kind of context it's then quite common to recap on what has gone before. This gives the characters some background history and also helps locate the present story in a time (and perhaps place). It enables the writer to efficiently slip in a few relevant facts and perhaps suggest motivation for the characters' future behaviour. This extract from the second page of *The Heat of Passion* is fairly typical:

'But it doesn't now,' Carlo traded softly. 'Now it belongs to me.'

Jessica's teeth gritted. Six years ago, burdened by the demands of a wife with expensive tastes, ageing machinery and falling profits, Gerald Amory had allowed Carlo to buy the family firm. Duly reinstalled as chief executive, her father had seemed content and, with new equipment and unparalleled export opportunities through the parent conglomerate, Amory Engineering had thrived.

Guilt stabbed like a knife into Jessica. If it had not been for her, Carlo Saracini would never have come into their lives. If it had not been for her, the firm would still have belonged to her father. If it had not been for her, Gerald Amory would not now be facing criminal charges for embezzlement. Nausea stirred in her stomach, churned up by a current of raw loathing so powerful, she could taste it.

'Dad intended to repay the money . . . if it hadn't have been for the audit, you wouldn't even have found out!' she blurted in desperation.

In this example we have been taken on a 'time out' from the present narrative. We can now locate references to 'six years ago' when they occur in the text. Jessica's feelings of guilt, too, have been foregrounded.

Another way of further exploring the mind of the main character is through the use of questions. These may act in three ways: first, they show the main character communing in a way with herself or himself; second, they establish a dialogue with the reader; and, third, they may be a way of providing moral comment. Again, some made-up examples will illustrate this:

How could she? thought Helen as she saw her best friend snog Mike.

But why me?

Where had the last few months gone?

After all, I wanted sex, and Tony had the hots for me big-time, so why not?

Why hadn't it occurred to her that, as the firm thrived and made all the money her greedy mother could ever have wanted, her father must have bitterly resented the fact that the firm was no longer his and that those healthy profits had come too late to sustain his shaky marriage?

The use of questions is a way of internalizing the point of view. They are the character's thoughts, reported directly or indirectly. They tend to be strong in feeling, expressing outrage, disbelief etc. Furthermore, they are used to moralize about the rights and wrongs of situations, past and future actions or the general fairness, or not, of life. They are especially important, too, because often the main character is isolated and communes with herself or himself, and they also allow the writer to engage in a kind of 'dialogue' with them.

Extension

For extension work pursue the various suggestions made throughout this unit.

And, now, to end, here is a complete short story written by Rosie Rushton for *Bliss* magazine. Do a complete analysis of it, looking for the features discussed above.

Heartbreaker

'An afternoon off - excellent!' Holly grabbed her beach towel, pushed her wraparound shades on top of her chestnut bob and shot herself an approving glance in the mirror suspended from the ceiling of the tent she shared with her friend Vicki.

'Too right!' agreed Vicki, slipping out of her campsite uniform to reveal a jungle print bikini. 'If I'd had to spend one more hour

---

organising games for that bunch of spoiled brats, I'd have jumped in the deep end myself!' Holly giggled.

'But it is worth it, isn't it?' she said. 'Being paid for six weeks of sand, sun and sea on the French coast.'

'And in your case, serious snogs,' added Vicki with a grin, yanking her red, wavy hair into a top-knot. 'And how is the delectable Scott?'

'Well fit,' said Holly. 'He is just such a total babe, isn't he? I'm going to meet him now - he's in the middle of teaching some kids to windsurf. Are you coming?'

'Definitely!' said Vicki. 'I reckon Jake's finally beginning to show a bit of interest. This bikini is designed to make him realise what a total fox he's got on his hands.' She grinned and flicked the shoestring strap of her tiny two piece.

'We ought to take Tara along,' suggested Holly, 'she's been so miserable since Paul left.'

'Where is she anyway?'

Vicki shrugged.

'Gone off on one of her lone walks, I think,' she said. 'Come on , let's go - I have some serious flirting to do!'

As they headed off through the pine trees at the end of the campsite, Holly thought about Tara. They had been best friends all through school, and when Holly hit on the idea of spending her year off working as a camp organiser at Les Pins Parasols in Brittany, she didn't think twice about asking her to come along too. Tara, who had just split up with her boyfriend, and was contemplating either jumping off a cliff or becoming a nun, perked up at the thought of a summer in the sun. She virtually bought her ferry ticket on the spot when Holly informed her that over half the camp entertainers were guys.

'Just the right place for falling in love,' she had said wistfully. One of Tara's ambitions was to be truly madly in love. Which, thought Holly, was why she had fallen so rapidly for Paul, the French bar man at Les Etoiles, the disco-bar. Within a week, she was telling anyone who would listen that this was the real thing. Paul, for his part, had plied her with free Belgian beer, taken her for moonlit rides on the back of his motorbike and told her she was 'très belle'. Tara had taken to practising writing Mrs Tara Challonier on scraps of paper and talking about when she'd meet his parents in Paris.

But the dream hit the dust last Saturday, when Paul and his bike disappeared, along with a sizeable portion of the week's bar profits. Since then, Tara had mooned around looking so soulful that Guy, the camp supervisor, had told her that she was there to keep the campers happy, not make them suicidal.

What Tara needed, thought Holly, was a nice guy who would make her feel special and stick with her through the summer. She wanted Tara to be as happy with someone as she was with Scott Carter.

'I reckon we ought to get Tara fixed up with Matt,' she said to Vicki as they crossed the sand dunes. 'He's about the only unattached boy left around here. How about tonight at the fancy dress barbecue? I could swap rotas so that Tara and Matt get to do the bar together.'

'Oh, come off it, Holly,' protested Vicki. 'You know Matt fancies you - he wouldn't look at anyone else. After all, it was him you chucked when Scott turned up on the scene.'

'I did not!' denied Holly hotly. 'You can't chuck someone when you were never an item. Is it my fault if he thought a couple of friendly dances was a licence to take possession?'

'You chatted him up like mad when we first got here,' said Vicki.

'I was just being friendly,' said Holly. 'After all, it can't be much fun being in charge of the Teddy Bear Club all day, can it? He's cute, but not my type,' she added, scanning the beach in vain for a sight of Scott, 'too square by far.'

'And Scott is Mr Perfect, I suppose,' grinned Vicki. 'Have you ... has he, well, you know?'

Holly smiled enigmatically.

'Wouldn't you like to know?' she said. She wasn't about to admit that, so far, Scott had been a nightmare. He hardly ever spoke to her when they were alone, then jumped all over her, expecting her to sleep with him.

She was pinning her hopes on the party that night; if she could lure Scott away from everyone else, she was sure she could get to know him better and feel a bit more comfortable about taking things further. He was everything that she fancied in a guy: tall, muscular, with surfy dishevelled hair and shoulders made for resting your head on.

From that first moment when he had turned from the bar and given her a slow, smouldering gaze from those incredible pewter-grey eyes, she was hooked.

She was certain that he felt the same - after all, he had ditched his previous girlfriend that very evening, getting off with Holly right in front of her. He'd allowed her to ride in his scarlet Mazda MX5 when he was making some deliveries in the town.

And when he put his hands on her leg and gave her a squeeze, Holly had nearly fainted with sheer blood-surging excitement.

Scott had it all. He'd won medals for windsurfing and, as well as being in charge of the camp's watersports activities, he gave tennis coaching (while Holly gawped at his tanned legs). The female campers on the site loved him. Holly still couldn't believe her luck in being the one girl to get him.

Even Tara, who had been out with practically the entire universe and had turned seduction into a fine art form, had failed to make an impression with Scott and was, Holly guessed, vaguely jealous.

Vicki and Holly reached the beach and flopped down on the sand.

'Look out,' warned Vicki, 'here comes lovestruck Matt.'

Matt caught sight of them and waved a hand as he ushered a group of kids up the beach.

'Just finished the sandcastle competition,' he said, brushing a stray lock of sandy hair out of his eyes. 'Timmy won.' A small boy with a sunburned nose and no front teeth grinned ecstatically. 'Now we're off for some chocolate pancakes.'

'Thrills,' muttered Holly sarcastically under her breath.

Matt beamed directly at Holly. 'Well, see you tonight then, at the fancy dress,' said Matt, looking at Holly. 'We're on the bar together.'

'I think I have to swap with Tara,' murmured Holly with what she hoped was a regretful smile. Matt flushed and his freckles stood out like full stops over his nose.

'Whatever ...' he said and drifted off, followed by a trail of chattering children.

'Heartbreaker,' teased Vicki. 'Come on, let's swim.'

'OK,' said Holly. 'But I must keep a lookout for Scott - he's promised to take me out on a jet ski this afternoon.'

It was while she was lying on her back, dreaming about that evening, and wondering whether the woods or the cave at the south end of the beach would be the best place for asking him if he loved her, that she spotted him. He was sitting on one of the rocks jutting out into the bay, knees pulled up to his chin, deep in conversation with someone. The sun was in Holly's eyes and she couldn't see who it was, but she guessed he was trying to find out where she had got to. She waved but he was looking the other way, so she swam towards the rocks. The current was against her and it took longer than she thought. When she finally got there, there was no sign of anyone. He'll have gone back to his tent, thought Holly. And if I just happened to be passing as he was changing out of his wet suit ...

She shivered with anticipation and headed for Scott's tent. The sun was dipping behind the trees, casting long shadows across the grass where the tables were already being set up for the party. Holly ran her fingers through her wet hair, slicked on some coconut lipgloss and stepped over the guy ropes. She was about to burst in and surprise him when she heard a voice from inside.

'But what about Holly?' The voice was unmistakably Tara's. Holly paused.

'Mmm? What about her? You smell lovely.'

'I don't think ... oh Scott!'

'It's OK, Holly thinks I'm madly in love with her, but it's you I've fancied for ages.'

Holly froze. It couldn't be. Of course, it wasn't.

Holly's heart was hammering in her chest and her mouth was suddenly dry. Surely, he couldn't ...? She pushed back the tent flap.

Scott was stretched out on the camp bed and lying in the crook of his arm, with eyes half-closed, was Tara.

Holly ran blindly. She couldn't bear it. Tara and Scott. Together. Scott was hers, he had said so. How could he? And how could Tara? She was supposed to be her friend. Just because she had lost Paul, she thought she could steal Holly's boyfriend. Well, we'd see about that.

'Holly, are you OK?' She collided with Vicki who was carrying a pile of fancy dress costumes.

Holly was about to tell her what had happened but she stopped. She wouldn't let anyone know. She couldn't stand the humiliation. And besides, there was still tonight. She would get Scott back.

'I'm fine,' said Holly, forcing herself to smile. 'Just fell over and hurt myself, that's all.'

A few hours later, Holly fixed a smile on her face and went over to where Scott was chatting to a few girls.

'He's not bad,' she heard one girl say. 'I wouldn't mind a windsurfing lesson with him.'

'I bet he's had more girls than you've had hot dinners. A girl in every tent,' she tittered.

Holly took a deep breath and gritted her teeth.

'Scott,' she said, letting her hair fall seductively over her face, 'how about you and me head for the beach?'

Scott gave a slow smile and looked intently into her eyes. Holly's heart leapt. But then he shook his head. 'No can do,' he said smoothly. 'Got to entertain the campers. Sorry.'

'But I could entertain you,' said Holly, trying to sound sophisticated and alluring. She reached out a hand and touched a strand of hair at the back of his neck, like she had seen Michelle Pfeiffer do in the movies.

'Look,' he said, 'if this is because of earlier ...'

'No,' said Holly, holding up her hand. 'I know what Tara's like - she comes on strong. I know it's me you love.'

She leaned slowly towards him. Scott drew back.

'Look don't tie me down, OK? It's over. Sorry.'

He turned and walked away. Holly didn't try to stop the tears. She didn't care about anything. How on earth would she survive the summer without Scott?

Somehow she got through the evening. Matt, looking faintly ridiculous in a clown costume with huge red shoes, had dragged her off to do the baby patrol.

'Why are you crying?' he had asked gently.

'I'm not!' Holly had snapped. 'It's pollen or something.'

Holly followed him round in a daze as he fetched mothers to yelling babies. It was on the third circuit, after Matt had finally appeased a three-year-old who had lost her teddy bear, that they saw them.

Scott and Tara, standing by the side of the pool. Holly stopped dead in her tracks and watched as Scott gently brushed a strand of blonde hair from Tara's eyes and cupped her face in his hands. Then, slowly, he put his lips to hers. Holly watched, incapable of turning away, as Tara linked her hands behind Scott's neck, closed her eyes, and kissed him slowly, passionately.

She cried so much she didn't have any tears left. She lost all sense of time but she knew it must be late. The full moon was shining on the sea and there wasn't a breath of air. The camp was silent; everyone was in their tents sleeping off the rough red wine that had been free all evening.

Holly had climbed onto the rocks and sat gazing at the sea. It had all gone wrong. Everything was over. She had lost the guy she loved and been betrayed by her best friend. She would be a laughing stock. She couldn't face them. Tomorrow she would give in her notice and go home to England. There was nothing left for her here.

She clambered back and jumped down onto the beach. A piercing needle-like pain shot through her foot. She screamed and dropped to her knees, grabbing her foot, but it was too dark to see what had happened.

She tried to walk but the pain was too bad. She sank down on the sand, put her head on her knees and cried out of tiredness, misery and sheer frustration.

'Hanky?'

Holly looked up. Matt was standing over her, still wearing his clown costume. He didn't ask her what was wrong. He simply sat down beside her, passed her a handkerchief and began throwing pebbles in the water.

After a few moments, he took her hand.

'It hurts like hell, doesn't it?' he said softly.

'Yes, I think I stood on a sharp stone,' sniffed Holly.

'No, not the foot,' said Matt. 'Being rejected, I mean.'

Holly gulped and nodded slowly.

'I've decided to go home,' she said miserably and waited for Matt to argue with her.

He appeared not to have heard. 'If it's any consolation, you're not the first,' he said. 'And it'll happen to Tara. Scott is that kind of guy. Likes the chase, hates the commitment.'

Holly said nothing.

'This is probably not the time to say this,' said Matt, staring with great concentration at his thumbnail, 'but you know how I feel about you. I know I'm nothing like Scott. I can never think of clever things to say until it's too late. That's why I like working with kids. They're more interested in chocolate buttons than chat-up lines.'

Holly smiled despite herself.

'Hey, that's a new one. I can make beautiful girls laugh,' he grinned.

'Am I beautiful?' asked Holly.

'Oh yes,' said Matt, 'far too beautiful for the likes of Scott Carter.'

And picking up her foot in his hand, he bent down and kissed it and stroked her ankle.

There were no chat-up lines, no witty one-liners. He just looked at her and smiled gently.

Then he picked her up in his arms and began carrying her up the beach.

'What are you . . .?'

'That foot needs cleaning up,' he said briskly, 'especially if you are off home tomorrow.'

'I didn't say,' said Holly, 'that I was going home for sure.'

'That's good,' said Matt. And he kissed her again.

It's remarkable, thought Holly, how a kiss can stop pain in the soul.

What is literature?

In considering the various points of view writers can adopt and also how they choose to represent character through speech and description, we have used extracts drawn from texts of various kinds, from the classics of Charles Dickens, Thomas Hardy and Jane Austen to the genre of detective fiction to the stream of consciousness writing of Jack Kerouac to the dialect writing of Irvine Welsh. In the last unit popular fiction writing was examined and its formulaic tendencies noted. There hasn't been space here to consider whether popular fiction should even be classed as literature. Obviously it is literature but how good, unique or timeless it is, is another question.

There has existed a feeling that for literature to be of high status it has to be difficult to read in some way; perhaps James Joyce's *Ulysses* is a classic example. But where does this place the writing, say, of Nick Hornby or Douglas Coupland, writing which is full of colloquialisms and Americanisms? And what about Welsh? The last unit, by exploring the formulaic style of some writing, its tendency to a clichéd, collocational language, did suggest that some texts could be considered less literary than others. And, conversely, texts considered of more merit might use language in a more innovative, unique or uplifting way. In the space that is left this last unit will consider what further questions might be asked of literature and how we might decide what makes a text literary.

Two general questions worth asking concern the expectations the reader brings to the text and the purpose behind the writing of the text. For example, a travel brochure or news story may be read to elicit facts; a novel read for pleasure. The primary purpose of a travel brochure may be to persuade, a news story to inform but the primary purpose of literature may arguably be to 'entertain' in its widest sense. The twin prongs of reader expectation and writer intention can be neatly illustrated by this rearrangement of the first line of a news item about Hell's Angels:

Most Angels are uneducated.
Only one
Angel in
ten
has
steady work.

from Herrnstein-Smith (1978: 67)

Here just by changing the lineation, this line of news suddenly seems more literary. It *looks* like poetry.

Activity

Take a few lines from a news item, a brochure or a guide and change their lineation. Do they now seem more 'poetic'? Consider also why menus and shopping lists are not normally thought of as being poetry. Can you take some examples and make them more poetic?

Here is another example; this is a rearrangement of a few lines from the
Official Guide for Frinton-on-Sea:

> Graciousness is the quality that gives
> Frinton
> on
> Sea
> a
> unique
> place
> among British holiday resorts.
> In the town's
> hotels and guest houses every visitor
> is regarded as
> an
> honoured
> guest.

Although a news item, or even a resort's official guide, might seem an
unusual source for a piece of literature, Ernest Hemingway wrote a short
story based on a news report which first appeared in The *New York Times*
on 20 December 1922, extract 1 here. Hemingway's story is then printed
as extract 2.* What does Hemingway leave out and what does he add?
What makes his story more literary than the news report?

*My attention was first drawn to these two extracts by their use in Simpson (1997:
102–27).

Extract 1

M. Gounaris, an ex-Premier, was in a hospital in a very critical condition. About 11 am he was taken out on a stretcher, placed in a motor van and driven to a place about one and a half miles outside of the city. He was left lying on his stretcher in a dying condition while the car went back to fetch five others from the prison where they had all been confined in a single room.

To begin the horrors of that morning it was discovered by the guards that one of the five had died in the van on the way out from heart failure.

On the arrival of the van Gounaris was lifted out of the stretcher to stand up and face a firing party. It was then found that this wretched man, who, after all, had been a figure in the recent history of Europe, was unable to stand at all. He was thereupon given sufficient injections of strychnine to strengthen the action of his heart to enable him to stand up in front of the firing party. The man who had died on the way out was propped up beside him - a ghastly line of four live men, one half alive and one dead man.

They were then asked - Gounaris, the dead man and all - if they had anything to say, an appalling instance of mockery. No reply was made, but M. Baltazzis took out his monocle, polished it and put it back again. General Hadjanestis calmly lit a cigarette. The order to fire was given. The moment the prisoners fell the firing party rushed forward and emptied their revolvers into the corpses. Including that of the man who had died on the way from the prison. The bodies were then thrown into a lorry and taken to a public cemetery just outside of the city and were thrown out casually in a heap in the mud which covered the ground.

Extract 2

They shot the six cabinet ministers at half past six in the morning against the wall of the hospital. There were pools of water in the courtyard. There were wet dead leaves on the paving of the courtyard. It rained hard. All the shutters of the hospital were nailed shut. One of the ministers was sick with typhoid. Two soldiers carried him downstairs and out into the rain. They tried to hold him up against the wall but he sat down in a puddle of water. The other five stood very quietly against the wall. Finally the officer told the soldiers it was no good trying to make him stand up. When they fired the first volley he was sitting down in the water with his head on his knees.

The most significant features of the news report are the narrative, which is chronologically structured, and the importance of facts, especially names, and detail. It's most of this detail which Hemingway leaves out and in its place we find timeless references to 'they'. The most startling addition concerns the rain and water – which may have been inspired by the 'mud' of the cemetery. Hemingway's story draws attention to itself largely through repetition. Many of the sentences are simple, having one main independent clause, and they have many instances of the verb 'to be' as well as the construction beginning 'they'. The most closely similar sentences are 'There were pools of water in the courtyard' and 'There were wet dead leaves on the paving of the courtyard' and this pattern is reinforced by their juxtaposition. There is also repetition at the lexical level: 'wall', 'courtyard' and most especially in the semantic field of 'water' which includes 'rain' and 'wet'. You might also have noticed the rather emotionless feel of the piece, largely achieved by the lack of adjectives; and where adjectives are used – 'wet dead leaves' – the unusual collocation of 'wet' with 'dead' again gives a poetic slant.

Fact or fiction?

The next two extracts are both largely concerned with description of place and the first, adapted from a travel brochure, is certainly *not* devoid of adjectives. Reader expectation of a travel brochure would be of finding facts, names and details. We would also expect an upbeat approach and expect to be sold something. Similarly, the intention behind the brochure would be to sell a product, a holiday and, without being deliberately misleading, give a gloss on what to expect. The second extract is from the opening of Anita Brookner's *Hotel du Lac*; readers won't normally come to this expecting to be sold a holiday in Vevey, on Lake Geneva.

Read the two extracts. Match and compare what each says about the same thing: for example, extract 1 talks of a 'lively, cosmopolitan atmosphere' but extract 2 mentions 'uncommunicative' and 'taciturn' inhabitants. Also write, in as much detail as you can, what you notice about the choice of language made in each as well as the sentence structure. Refer also to the overall structure of extract 2.

Extract 1
Lake Geneva

Enjoying an unusually mild climate, this beautiful lake region has a lively, cosmopolitan atmosphere. The serene waters of this immense lake are banked by gentle hillsides covered in vineyards and gardens. Visitors will be dazzled by the choice of places of interest to visit, either by boat, bus or train.

Vevey

Situated between Montreux and Lausanne on the lakeside, Vevey is an attractive market town, with cobbled streets and interesting little shops, cafés and restaurants. Smaller than its two neighbours, it benefits from a very regular boat service to all the interesting places on the lake. The village centre is very quaint, with regular markets and folklore festivals taking place. And Vevey is steeped in history, having been a favourite of many famous visitors - Hemingway, Byron and Chaplin amongst them. You are bound to visit the 13th century Castle of Chillon on the lakeside, immortalised by the poet Byron.

Vevey is the starting point for several enchanting walks, and also for some lovely steam and funicular train journeys which afford wonderful views of the lake and surrounding countryside.

Please note: The steamer service on Lake Geneva is significantly reduced from around 20 September.

Hotel du Lac

Location: Ideally situated on Vevey's lakeside promenade with dramatic views across to the French Alps dominated by the lofty Dent d'Oche peak.

Extract 2
From the window all that could be seen was a receding area of grey. It was to be supposed that beyond the grey garden, which seemed to sprout nothing but the stiffish leaves of some unfamiliar plant, lay the vast grey lake, spreading like an anaesthetic towards the invisible further shore, and beyond that, in imagination only, yet verified by the brochure, the peak of the Dent d'Oche, on which snow might already be slightly and silently falling. For it was late September, out of season; the tourists had gone, the rates were reduced, and there were few inducements for visitors in this small town at the water's edge, whose

inhabitants, uncommunicative to begin with, were frequently rendered taciturn by the dense cloud that descended for days at a time and then vanished without warning to reveal a new landscape, full of colour and incident: boats skimming on the lake, passengers at the landing stage, an open air market, the outline of the gaunt remains of a thirteenth-century castle, seams of white on the far mountains, and on the cheerful uplands to the south a rising backdrop of apple trees, the fruit sparkling with emblematic significance. For this was a land of prudently harvested plenty, a land which had conquered human accidents, leaving only the weather distressingly beyond control.

Commentary

The abundance of complimentary adjectives stands out in the travel brochure. In just the first few lines we read:

mild
beautiful
lively
cosmopolitan
serene
immense
gentle

and when these are exhausted the writing resorts to almost content-less adjectives such as 'interesting', 'lovely' and 'wonderful'. Actually the opening description has a nice contrast: *mild* versus *lively*; *serene and gentle* versus *immense*.

What perhaps is most interesting about this writing though, is its similarity to some of the features of popular fiction which were discussed in Units 5 and 6. First, there is the use of collocations. We find, for example:

mild climate
serene waters
cobbled streets
steeped in history
immortalised by the poet.

There is, also, an extended metaphor to emphasise effect, when describing the Dent d'Oche: 'dominated ... lofty ... peak'. Finally, some of the sentences display the formulaic structure of popular fiction. This is the device of participle clause followed by the main clause and which has the effect of shifting the focus to the subject – italicised here:

> Enjoying an unusually mild climate, *this beautiful lake region* has a lively, cosmopolitan atmosphere.

> Situated between Montreux and Lausanne on the lakeside, *Vevey* is an attractive market town, with cobbled streets and interesting little shops, cafes and restaurants.

> Smaller than its two neighbours, *it* benefits from a very regular boat service to all the interesting places on the lake.

By contrast, Anita Brookner's extract might almost be a direct response to the promises offered by the travel brochure. The avoidance of collocations gives a freshness and uniqueness to the writing, for example, 'gaunt remains' and 'cheerful uplands'. The repetition of 'grey' in the first three lines reinforces the absence of a view and leads neatly into the unusual simile 'like an anaesthetic'. There is also the arresting coinage of a 'grey garden'. The overall structure, too, is interesting. There are just four sentences, the second two balancing and answering the question of the weather posed by the first two. There is also a cohesive link with the second two sentences starting with 'For'. The first sentence introduces the grey view which is extended into the next sentence. The long and complex third sentence explains the reason for the view – because it was 'late September'; then, suddenly, the clouds go and a new vista appears. The final sentence comments on this: this is a land which can control everything but not the weather.

Some features, then, of literature noticed in the short story of Hemingway and the extract from Brookner are those of repetition – both lexical and at the level of the sentence. There is also the use of fresh or unusual collocation and an overall awareness of structure. It is often easier to explain non-literary pieces and work of lower literary status. Texts considered to be worthy of merit are often so because of their freshness – and this is harder to categorize.

This unit will close with an extract from Jonathan Raban's *Coasting*, which has been described as 'half travel book, half autobiography, half novel'. Here he describes a meeting with the poet Philip Larkin in the city of Hull. What kind of writing would you describe this as? The dubious arithmetic of the quote above reflects the problem. In what ways could it be considered literary? Note there is no commentary.

Among the jaunty salesmen in the lobby of the Royal Station Hotel, I looked out for Philip Larkin and eventually found his long, pale face, like a fugitive white barn owl caught in unaccustomed daylight. He was evidently prepared for all eventualities this evening. Although the temperature outside was in the sixties, he wore a winter overcoat and knotted scarf, and carried a furled brolly. He was beaming shyly, shortsightedly, and not quite in my direction. I planted myself in the centre of the beam.

'Ah, there you are. It was the hat that threw me.'

'I always wear a hat now I'm going bald.'

Larkin's own large skull was as hairless as a cheese.

'Yes, I used to go in for hats once, too. I never found they did any *permanent* good.'

At the bar, he asked for a gin and tonic. 'Would you mind making that a double gin? Since I've gone so deaf, I don't seem to be able to *see* single gins any more.'

As we sat down he said, 'I'm a great deal deafer than I was when I last saw you,' but the tone in which this was said, and the expression which accompanied it, suggested that a marked improvement in his health had taken place.

Larkin was wired for sound, with a conspicuous pink appliance lodged in each ear. His hearing aids, his thick glasses, the doughy rolls of smooth white flesh on which his chin rested in repose, all had the accentuated reality of theatrical props. It was as if he took a melancholy, ironic satisfaction in advertising to the world just how far his worst fears about himself had already been confirmed.

Extension

1   Rearrange the lines from a text which is not poetry, say from a news report, a town guide or a travel brochure so that it looks like poetry. Show them to others. Find some poetry by e. e. cummings. How important are the lay-out and the expectations readers bring to the work?

2   Use a news item as the basis for a short story, along the lines of Hemingway. What do you leave out and what do you add? How do you make it literary?

3   Do some investigating into the narrative employed by newspaper articles. If they are not chronologically oriented, then why not? You could start by comparing sports reports, say of soccer matches, in tabloids and broadsheets.

4   Take some travel brochures. Use them as a basis for the setting of a short story.

5   Finally, look at some writing which isn't fiction but can be considered literature in its widest sense, for example autobiographies and travel books. Do they share any of the features of prose fiction? Can they be explored following the categories employed in this book? You could start by looking at Sylvia Plath's *The Bell Jar* or some of the travel writing of Bill Bryson.

index of terms

This is a form of combined glossary and index. Listed below are some of the main key terms used in the book, together with brief definitions for purposes of reference. The page references will take you to the first use of the term in the book where it is shown in **bold**. In some cases, however, understanding of the term can be helped by exploring its uses in more than one place in the book and accordingly more than one page reference is given.

Not all terms used are glossed here as a limited number of terms in the book receive extensive discussion and explanation in particular units. This is also by no means a full index of linguistic terms so it should be used in conjunction with other books, dictionaries and encyclopaedias which are indicated in the Further Reading section. For a more detailed explanation of the terms used in the book, see the glossary to *Working With Texts: A core book for language analysis.*

the subject, here italicised: 'Angered by the noise, *he* strode to the balcony'; 'Squaring her shoulders, *she* pressed the doorbell'.

phonological 51

To do with the sound of words; see also 'eye dialect'.

point of view 4

First mentioned in Unit 1 but see Units 2 and 3.

stream of consciousness 13

Also known as the internal monologue: a stream of words to suggest loosely associated thought. See, too, Jack Kerouac's spontaneous prose, also on p. 14.

syntactic 51

The vocabulary and grammar used here to indicate features of a dialect.

unmarked vocabulary 76

Also referred to as 'core vocabulary'; these are words which are neutral, so 'say' rather than 'purr', 'murmur', etc.; 'blue' rather than 'ultramarine', 'smoky turquoise', etc.

voice 4

Used to describe the way a writer seems to be speaking to the reader; first introduced in Unit 1 but then used throughout the book. Not to be confused with active and passive voice. See also the different voices employed by David Lodge in *Therapy*, pp. 25-28.

index of texts discussed

further reading

A good place to start would be to read some of the complete texts from which extracts have been taken; whether this means going back to texts you have met before or unknown ones probably doesn't matter.

As far as following up other books on the issues discussed here, then for a general and wide-ranging perspective, which also encompasses language varieties and narrative in film, try:

Montgomery, Martin, Alan Durant, Nigel Fabb, Tom Furniss and Sara Mills (1992) *Ways of Reading*, London, Routledge.

Another wide-ranging book which, amongst other things, covers language in travel brochures, as well as language in newspapers and adverts - but don't be put off by the cover - is:

Carter, Ron and Walter Nash (1990) *Seeing Through Language*, Oxford, Blackwell.

For a book which poses some interesting questions, including sections on accent and dialect, pop fiction and gender, try:

Hackman, Sue and Barbara Marshall (1990) *Re-reading Literature*, London, Hodder & Stoughton.

Another book for those wishing to further explore detailed analysis on language and gender is, as the title suggests:

Mills, Sara (1995) *Feminist Stylistics*, London, Routledge.

The book to read for further analysis of pop fiction, including 'stories for boys' (and written in a very personal style) is:

Nash, Walter (1990) *Language in Popular Fiction*, London, Routledge.

For more in-depth discussion on literary language, cohesion in narrative structures and especially if you want to follow up Hemingway's use of The *New York Times* article then look to:

Simpson, Paul (1997) *Language Through Literature*, London, Routledge.

Two more books which are very detailed and probably ones to dip into are:

Fowler, Roger (1986) *Linguistic Criticism*, Oxford, Oxford University Press.

Leech, Geoffrey and Michael Short (1981) *Style in Fiction*, London, Longman.

And, finally, either a good place to finish or just for a break, try any collections of:

Calvin and Hobbes by Bill Watterson.

references

Carter, Ron (1987) *Vocabulary: Applied Linguistic Perspectives,* London, Allen & Unwin.

Nash, Walter (1990) *Language in Popular Fiction,* London, Routledge.

Herrnstein-Smith, B. (1978) *On the Margins of Discourse: The Relation of Language to Literature,* Chicago, University of Chicago Press.